PATH
TO
POWER

PATH
TO
POWER

It's All in Your Mind

Roger Heisler

SAMUEL WEISER, INC.
York Beach, Maine

First published in 1990 by
Samuel Weiser, Inc.
Box 612
York Beach, Maine 03910

Library of Congress Cataloging-in-Publication Data

Heisler, Roger A. 1949–
    Path to power : it's all in your mind / Roger A. Heisler.
        p.   cm.
    1. Magic. I. Title
    BF1611.H47   1990
    133.4'3—dc20   90-38636
                                              CIP
  ISBN 0-87728-705-8

Cover photography: "Mother Nature," © Stephen King, 1990
used by permission of Fisikon, Schwanenhof D-6759
Wolfstein, W. Germany.
Typeset in 11 point Goudy by
World Composition Services, Inc.
Printed in the United States of America by
Edward Brothers, Inc.

To Toni W.
who has listened to me and argued with me in friendship
for more years than I deserve.

Contents

Acknowledgments

Many thanks to Hal and Sandy, who got me started; to Carol Ann, who provided the motivation to keep me going; and to Dixie, whose ears and input were invaluable in completing this book.

PATH
TO
POWER

God has made different religions to suit different aspirants, times and countries. All doctrines are only so many paths; but a path is by no means God itself. Indeed, one can reach God if one follows any of the paths with whole-hearted devotion.

Gospel of Sri Rama Krishna
Translated by Swami Nikhilananda

CHAPTER ONE

The Basics of Power

POWER.

Welcome to a taste of power. And knowledge. This is a book about power, and how to use it to benefit yourself and others. To some extent, this book is about religion and philosophy, but it's not a religious book and doesn't preach. Instead, we start with a premise held by mystics and occultists— that the three paths to awareness are love, knowledge and power.

Let's start with a working definition of power that we can use here: Power is energy manipulated to perform work. That's not exactly a proper scientific definition, but it suits our purposes. We want to tap into sources of energy you may not have been using and show you how to direct that energy with your mind to do something, obtain something, or influence something.

The kind of power we're discussing involves the ability to cause deliberate change in the world around you through non-physical means. This could be virtually any kind of change: a change in the weather, a change in lifestyle, a change in health, a change in attitude. This power causes an alteration in the existence of someone or something around you, but it's not a random alteration. Rather, the change is made according to what you want—what you have in mind as a picture of how things should be—in accordance with your will. Change is brought about through non-physical means: with your mind rather than your hands.

Now, that doesn't sound very spooky, does it? I hope not, because it happens to be a good working definition of magick, which really isn't anything to be too frightened of. Power is power, and if you don't handle it properly, something could go wrong and you could get burned. Or worse. Not that this power is very hard to understand or difficult to control, it just takes some time and practice. I recommend that you take time to read and study before getting too carried away with all the possibilities (or your own fantasies). Don't get the idea you can put this book down ten minutes from now and zap someone. You *might* be able to do it, but probably not too well, not too effectively, and not too safely.

This book is intended to provide some basic guidelines on what it takes to do magick. It's a primer, not a definitive work. It would take many volumes to cover every detail of each aspect that contributes to reaching a person's full potential of efficiency and effectiveness. Actually, it can take a fairly impressive library to cover everything—ask anyone who's been involved with magick for a while. They'll tell you. When you're ready for more detailed information on breathing or nutrition or mythology or talismans or sigils or whatever, go out and get another book specializing in that particular area. Any book store can order any book you want if it's still in print. The list of suppliers in the back of this book can also help you with anything else you may need. (This resource list is hardly definitive, but it's a starting point.)

So this book is a guide. It contains pointers, ideas, suggestions and general direction intended to communicate important, basic concepts behind magick and the Craft. It's not too advanced and, hopefully, it's simple enough to be a good starting point for anybody. While you may not find all the detail you want on any particular subject, you should come away with sufficient understanding to be able to better judge the validity and accuracy of anything else you read, and that's extremely valuable.

Spiritual Development

Most people in the field believe that to gain magickal power and knowledge you have to reach a certain level of spiritual development. In theory, there are three paths to spiritual awakening, development and evolution. Two, knowledge and power, are supposed to go hand-in-hand with spiritual development, and this is often true. The third element is love. I don't take issue with that, but the emphasis generally has been exclusively on the path of love as though nothing else existed. Some say that without love for mankind, nature and all of creation, nothing else will get you anywhere spiritually. Some may say that, but it's an incomplete, misleading, limiting, defeatist attitude to hold.

The Qabalah contains what's called "The Tree of Life." You've probably seen pictures of it—a series of circles at different levels connected with lines. Each of the circles represents an aspect of life and spiritual development, and the lines are the pathways we follow from the bottom to the top. Most people think of this as a continuous pathway from the bottom sephiroth (or sphere) through each of the others until the top is reached, indicating exposure to and mastery of every aspect of life on this plane. What they tend to forget is that the spheres are arranged in three columns, rather than in a single vertical column, and the pathways go up through these columns. In other words, you can advance through a column with minimal exposure to most of the other stops along the way. Also, the various sephirah are connected to each other by other paths, making it possible to progress from bottom to top in any one of a number of different ways, taking each in turn or skipping some entirely. The long way around is slower and easier, no doubt, yet it's not the *only* way there. The tree demonstrates this fact very well.

Still, you have to start somewhere, and usually you just start with what you have. An open, healthy love of everything in creation would be an unusual place to expect most of us to start. However, you can develop that attitude in time. Forgetting about infatuations, love generally requires time, knowledge and understanding to grow. It rarely happens overnight (regardless of how that night is spent).

Knowledge and power are the two other paths open to us, and they go together in many ways. With greater knowledge comes the potential for more power (if the desire is in that direction), and as our power increases we learn more, understand more, and find more sources of additional information available. Hopefully, as you learn more and develop increased powers, you will spend more time contemplating life and appreciating the nature, source and capabilities of the forces at work, all of which will contribute to making you a wiser person.

Greater power has a history of leading to greater knowledge. Early in human history, most (if not all) human existence was centered around the necessity of finding food, which didn't leave time for much else. As people learned to domesticate plants and animals as food sources (developing power over their environment), they spent less time searching for sustenance, which left more time for other things, such as observing and contemplating the world. This change resulted in the development of astronomy, along with an alphabet, mathematics, music, art and architecture.

With greater material sufficiency, there is more free time; with more free time, there is more observation and learning; with more learning, there is greater knowledge and understanding of the universe; with greater knowledge and understanding, people gain more power and influence over the universe. And so humanity progresses and evolves.

Think back to all of the artists, composers, musicians, scientists, and philosophers you can recall. Many were paid well for the work they did or had patrons to support them, though by the 19th century patronage wasn't what it had once been. Some artists occasionally had to produce works they didn't really want to do. I'm sure Michelangelo and daVinci from time to time found it necessary to do something on commission because they needed food rather than because they felt inspired. Mozart certainly did. But the best works resulted from desire, opportunity and choice.

It's hard to be spiritual when you're hungry. Lots of people do it, but it's not easy. Our Western culture doesn't condition us psychologically to accept being hungry as a natural part of life. When we have what we need to be comfortable, we tend to put our minds to more lofty matters. While some may argue otherwise, we *do* have an obligation to ourselves to be happy, comfortable and generally well-off, while maintaining the search for higher spiritual levels. There's nothing wrong with using *all* of the powers given to us in order to obtain that end of being comfortable.

Material things do not distract us from the path; we are distracted by the ceaseless desire and quest for the acquisition of more and more, beyond what we need or can even use. Good, comfortable, warm clothes are a necessity; a decent car can be a necessity; a safe, clean, comfortable place to live is a necessity. A mink coat, BMW and condo in the Virgin Islands may be nice, but they're not necessities on the same level as having a job you enjoy. I find it hard to picture reading the Qabalah and shooing away rats at the same time.

Avoid excesses. It's okay to use magick to get a good job that will support you well while you enjoy doing it. However, using magick to get rid of a superior so you can get a promotion you don't really need or deserve is another thing. Materialism as a way of life is bad; wanting to be comfortable is not. Once immediate needs are satisfied, the mind can then turn to higher priorities. This will gradually lead to a greater understanding of people and life—another step on the path of love. Power can lead to knowledge, and power plus knowledge can lead to love; ultimately, all three paths work together. There's no reason why you can't choose the path of power and improve your lot in life before worrying about spiritual matters.

No doubt some will read this book, follow its logic, reference other sources, and try to develop their magickal abilities just for the sake of power and personal gain. These are the people most books and groups try to discourage, if not ostracize outright. You shouldn't make value judgments on what another individual needs to develop, and I don't care to judge who can or cannot, will or will not, gain something useful that might change a negative attitude into a more positive one. I'm reasonably certain eventually we all will get what we deserve. So if the information here becomes the trigger for someone's evil future, they'll end up paying for it.

There's work to be done, and some of it will require detached power more than involved love. It's said that love can move mountains, but I'd rather depend on the Army Corps of Engineers. Depending on what you're trying to accomplish, love may be the best tool, but sometimes it takes power. Some of the work we face requires a power different from that obtained through love. Some of you reading this may find your way to that working place and help all of us.

Religion and the Role of Rituals

This process has more than a little to do with religion. That may cause some of you a little trouble because I'm referring to the "old religion." Wicca. Paganism. (Sometimes referred to as Neo-paganism.) Not that you have to be a pagan or Wiccan or anything else to use this, but it helps, since certain philosophical attitudes and beliefs will help you work magick. If you feel in your heart an affinity for any particular aspect mentioned here, so much the better. If not, treat it as part of the experiment in learning—a test of a working theory or an operating system. (It isn't necessary, for instance, to accept the traditional explanation of the nature of electricity for you to be able to turn on a light.) It may be harder for a confirmed atheist to work with this, but it can be done.

Most of the ideas here have been used in some form or other by just about everyone who has ever used any kind of magick and much of it has been borrowed through the years by other, more traditional religions for worship ceremonies. In turn, some of it has been borrowed back again in its new form.

I'd like to offer the following truisms, truths, sayings, observations, and other words of relevance for your consideration and edification:

- Thinking generates energy. The more concentration put into a thought, the more energy is generated.

- There are planes of existence other than our own.

- If enough energy is put into a particular thought, that energy can bring the thought into reality on another plane and, in turn, create a similar reality on the physical plane. ("As Above, so Below.")

- Once enough energy has been put into a thought to give it form, additional energy directed at the form beyond what's required to sustain it will be stored in the form. This stored energy can be tapped by the human mind. In other words, the form becomes like a battery, drawing energy to charge itself, then storing excess energy in such a way that it can be drawn on later when needed or desired.

- Through the centuries people have created many deities and pantheons, and a lot of people have put a lot of energy into prayers, rites, rituals, ceremonies and sacrifices directed at these gods and goddesses.

- If these deities didn't have an existence before they were worshipped, they do now.

- Magick is all in your mind.

Having said all that, I have laid the groundwork for everything else. All things start in the mind. If you can focus on an idea with enough force, you can eventually bring that idea into existence. If you have trouble doing that, you can tap into the energy stored in any of the gods, goddesses, saints, demons, or elementals from any time in history. Millions of people have stored energy with their deities that you can draw on.

I'm not necessarily taking the position that every deity ever worshipped originated as a figment of someone's imagination. Many probably had real, physical existences in our world at one time, and others may have already existed without ever having a physical presence, but for the sake of making the following material easier for the unbeliever to accept, taking the position that they're people's creations is preferable to extensive occult and metaphysical debating.

Magick is the ability to bring about changes in people or situations in accordance with will through non-physical means. Non-physical implies the use of energy of some kind, and that's the root of magick. It involves the concentration of energy, then the direction of that energy to accomplish a particular end result. The direction of energy is accomplished through the will. No ritual, no tools will make you successful if you can't focus your attention on what it is you want to do to the exclusion of everything else, and then pour your energy into it.

The source of that energy is your own mind, plus the energy drawn into you from all that's around you, the physical world and/or the Universal All. The key lies in your own mind. Much of the energy comes from your own being; additional energy can't be absorbed from around you without the use of your mind.

How do you concentrate the energy and send it out to do what you want it to? One way is through concentration and meditation. Think about what it is you wish to accomplish. Focus all your attention on that one thing and picture it happening: visualization. Make the image sharp in your mind. As you concentrate all of your attention on that image, you start putting energy into it.

If the concentration of energy is all in your head, what are the rituals and tools for? Little of the brain is ever used, and most of what is used is used rarely. The problem is to open up additional portions of the brain-mind in order to produce and/or attract the needed energy. In this area the working tools and rituals become valuable, acting as mental triggers to aid concentration. None of these things are absolutely indispensable. The accomplished witch (a pagan, male or female, knowledgeable in the ways of magick) or magician (a practitioner of ceremonial or ritual magick) can operate with nothing but the mind itself. Also, repeating myself, your efforts will not succeed if you can't concentrate all your energy into what you're trying to accomplish.

A great deal of psychology comes into play here. People need ritual, plain and simple. Few, if any, religions lasted that did not have some ritual element in them. Ritual creates an atmosphere conducive to what you're trying to do, whether it be praying or working magick. Ritual brings a degree of order into what may otherwise seem to be a chaotic environment; by following the pre-set steps of a ritual, your mind goes deeper and more into what it's doing, aiding concentration and generating more energy. (Ritual is a form of self-hypnosis, actually.) Until you can sit down wherever you are and achieve complete concentration of thought on your objective at will, you would be well advised to take advantage of the psychological benefits of using ritual in your work.

The working tools, which we will discuss later, also serve as psychological triggers. For instance, a magician I know has a particular robe he uses for certain kinds of magick. In fact, he has a different robe for each basic type of magickal work. This man is accomplished in magick to the point that he doesn't need to use any tools or rituals at all, but it's always desirable to use as little energy and effort as necessary to accomplish what you want. Through repeated usage, his mind has become programmed to associate a particular robe with a particular magickal ritual. Because of this programming, the mere act of putting on a particular robe triggers the portion of his mind that he uses to perform his work. This area of the mind could be opened up by concentration and will, of course, but the conditioning (auto-hypnosis) associated with putting on the robe opens it up right away with far less effort and time.

Likewise, the athame (black-handled knife) is used in almost every magick ritual. The mind becomes programmed to the idea that every time you pick up that athame you're going to be doing magick of some sort. Since from past experience the mind already knows what state it must be in to do this work, picking up that athame triggers the mind into that state automatically. You can reach that state without the athame as a trigger, but once the mind becomes programmed to associate the athame with magick, and magick with a certain state of mind, the athame will act as a trigger that will save you time and effort. The same principle holds true with all of your working tools and various paraphernalia. Each will act as a trigger, helping you to prepare for your work much faster and with less effort.

Another reason for ritual is simply the fact that it's based on what others have done before you. In a way, ritual is a path that has been beaten by hundreds of thousands (or even millions) of people over many centuries and it's going your way. Following the established pathway will take a lot less energy than trying to create a new path of your own. Following the well-trodden path will make your work easier, especially in the beginning, and provide the basics of how to work. After that, you're on your own.

From time to time throughout this book you'll find the word *experiment.* You've got to experiment, but you're expected to learn the basics first. Is magick a science? It is certainly similar to physics in that it studies the generation, manipulation, application and control of energy. A primary difference, of course, is that the energy in question here has no identifiable physical source, nor can it be measured by any instruments invented yet. It also has connections to the social sciences. A sociologist, for instance, can probably understand much of the purely ritual nature of practicing magick, and a psychologist will probably appreciate much of the auto-hypnosis and other psychological considerations that comprise magick.

While we don't have instruments to detect and measure the energies utilized in performing magick, successful magickal acts are subject to verification and replication. If something works, you can see that it works and you should be able to repeat both the process and the effects again. These are two key elements to earning the label of science. The main element that's lacking is a tangible way to generate or detect the energy in question. This shortcoming doesn't seem to matter with psychology, however; it's considered a science. I think this failure to consider magick objectively is a little unfair and does nothing more than promote the religious prejudices of the past.

Some of you probably already practice magick or have demonstrated some type of psychic ability. Hopefully, others will be able to do so once you start using the ideas in this book. I ask all of you to come out of the closet. Ignorance and fear are the two greatest obstacles to progress. If you hide what you can do, people will remain ignorant of the possibilities and, if ever confronted with them, may respond with fear or violence. And your own fear of discovery isn't doing anything positive for you, either.

I'm not advocating grandstanding. Don't go climbing up on a stage claiming to be a psychic, witch or magician, telepath or clairvoyant or anything else. If a reasonable opportunity occurs to use your abilities, use them openly. If someone is tongue-tied over something and you can pick up on what it is, say it. If you can see what's going to happen to someone in the future, go ahead and say something instead of worrying about being embarrassed if you're wrong. If they ask something like "what are you, a mind-reader?" just answer "yes," smile, walk away and let it go at that. If someone needs help with something and you think a magickal act might be just the answer, say you're going to try to help, then perform the magick. If it does work and you're asked about it, admit to just what you did. Never take on public demonstrations, but use your power naturally and don't try to hide it. (If you could do large mathematical computations in your head you'd do them when appropriate but wouldn't care about wasting your time on meaningless demonstrations.)

At first you might be laughed at. Later, you might see people watching you out of the corners of their eyes with suspicion; you may even run into some hostility. Accept it. If you don't make a big thing out of what you're doing and just treat it like any other natural ability, eventually people will accept it and let it go. Once people start accepting this ability in others as part of their day-to-day existence, the curse of prejudice will be broken.

•   •   •

We're going to look at a couple of different, basic systems of magick—Wicca and Ceremonial—and how the power of magick can be used to improve your life. Many aspects of the philosophy of which ceremonial magick is a part can be very important later on, but are too advanced for beginners and, hence, will not be covered here. This book isn't meant to give you a whole new perspective on creation and how the universe works; it's intended to introduce you to a new source of power and to teach you how to develop that power in yourself, how to avail yourself of more power from outside yourself and how to work with that power once you've begun to develop it.

With that, we're first going to look at sources of power.

CHAPTER TWO

Sources of Power

I'M GOING TO APPROACH the subject of sources of power from four directions: personal, natural, psychic and universal. These classifications are somewhat arbitrary, but they'll help make things clearer for you. You should understand the types of power and some of the characteristics and peculiarities of each before you actually try to use them. They're not all that easy to define, but let's try.

Where does all of this power we're talking about come from? Nature is a big part of the answer. Everything comes from somewhere, and whether you believe that somewhere to be a supreme being, or just nature, isn't all that important. We're born with some of this power, we have access to unlimited quantities of it, and everything around us is permeated with it and connected by it.

The fact we can't scientifically identify the energy involved shouldn't trouble you too much. As time goes on, physicists continue to identify additional types of forces in the universe. For instance, it used to be that electro-magnetic, gravitational and strong and weak nuclear forces were the only types recognized by science, but now there's something being called "hypercharge." In time there will be more. Just ask any knowledgeable physicist. I'm confident that eventually they'll identify the forms of energy utilized in telepathy, clairvoyance, magick, and the energy which makes up "ghosts." (There may be some trouble quantifying it, but that's just another puzzle to be solved.)

Universal energy is all around us. The creative energy of the universe is in all things, in all places at all times. It's prana, it's the white light, and it's limitless in its quantity. This universal energy exists independent of man and nature, but is essential to all life.

Psychic energy could be considered an aspect of the universal energy, or an aspect of personal energy, or a combination of both, or none of the above. For the purpose of this discussion, we're going to treat it as a little of both and something more.

Psychic energy is, in part, an energy found in life on other planes (including the planes of angels and demons), rather than free-floating universal energy. Also, it's a personal human energy that can be made to manifest in various forms on other planes. Sometimes referred to as thought forms, these can range in nature from the deities of ancient pantheons to familiars created today. It's the energy that people have sent into the universe with specific, detailed visualizations giving the energy form and substance of a type that can maintain itself. Like the universal energy, psychic energy can be drawn upon at any time; unlike the universal energy, psychic energy can only be drawn upon through the images, attributes and conditions by which the forms were originally created and recognized.

Natural energy is different. Its source is nature. It's energy that comes from the sun, the moon and the earth, from trees, rivers and fields. If you're sensitive enough, you can feel the energy that resides in a tree, for instance, or is created by a flowing river. You can draw on this energy like any other form of energy. It waxes and wanes with the sun, moon and seasons. It's all around us, but dependent on our environment. Destroy the forests, fields and animal life on the planet, and there will be little natural energy left. Conversely, the more life there is, the more energy there is.

Personal Power

Personal energy is what you generate inside of yourself—the chemical energy that keeps your body and brain functioning, as well as your mental energy, psychic energy and sexual energy. You often exercise all these forms of energy together. When making love, for instance, all of them come into play at once, as is true in some religious rituals.

Personal energy is not limitless; it depends on many different factors, including your physical condition. The healthier you are the more energy you have. Yet some people have a narrow view of health and don't fully realize its significance. The human body has a fantastic ability to maintain itself and to correct imbalances. We inhale and ingest vast quantities of poisons—carbon monoxide, nicotine, artificial preservatives—every day, and usually our bodies just cleanse the toxins from our systems.

The body's cleansing system, as well as the basic maintenance system, consumes energy. The less excess weight (fat) we carry, the less energy our bodies need to maintain themselves. In the process of cleansing and healing itself, the body directs energy to specific areas in need of attention. If we could breathe only clean air, we would expend far less energy keeping our lungs clean and the rest of our bodies free of air-borne toxins. Likewise, if we could eat only "pure" food, our bodies would use less energy keeping our blood and various organs clean and working at maximum efficiency.

To keep the body going well in spite of how most of us live takes a lot of energy. Some people can handle all of that with little difficulty; others use an inordinate amount of personal energy keeping the body functioning at all.

Everything in nature seeks a balance. When something is out of balance, for whatever reason, nature attempts to reestablish the balance. That takes energy. The more out of balance the body becomes, the more energy it requires and diverts in an attempt to regain its balance. All the energy your body has to use to correct itself is unavailable for other applications. On the other hand, if you were to eat more intelligently, exercise more and generally limit the quantity of undesirable substances in your body, the energy you save could be put to other uses. (If your body is in better balance, the energy you have is utilized more efficiently, so you need less to function, you can eat less and save money.)

Nature seeks a balance. That's a given fact of life. If our ecosystem was in balance we would have better quality air, cleaner water, more life, more energy and less interference to overcome in magickal work. If our bodies and minds were completely balanced we, too, would be healthier and happier. And we'd probably live longer. However, if everything were in balance, our tendency would be to maintain that static condition.

While it may sound like a paradox, there should be a balance between "balanced" and "imbalanced" conditions. When there is an imbalance, nature uses whatever means are available to bring things into balance and frequently designs new ways of doing it. Imbalance creates a dynamic situation in which energies are brought into play to alter existing conditions, ultimately creating something new and/or different. Imbalance produces change, and change is the heart of evolution. The greater the imbalance, the greater the motivation to regain balance, and the greater the likelihood of succeeding. Throughout history the efforts of a few dynamic individuals to change things has pulled the rest of the race along toward spiritual as well as material development. Within our own physical world, imbalance is a necessary, driving force.

Now let's get back to the matter of personal energy.

Energy *flows*. It isn't static. At least, it should flow. If it's static, it's only potential energy.

The Eastern philosophies speak of the body's energy flow with reference to the chakras. Chakras are a series of energy centers in the body running from the groin, up the spine to the top of the head. Each chakra relates to a specific area of the body. When the chakras are all in balance, energy flows from bottom to top through them. This energy flow is called kundalini, a Sanskrit word meaning "coiled up," and is usually depicted as a serpent coiled between the anus and genitals that slowly unwinds, working its way up the spine.

Kundalini and the chakras have been written about widely and can be researched in depth. It can be a complete study just by itself, and requires a great deal of work, but the results can be very rewarding. The sense of physical well-being, energy and power will do a lot for you.

If the body is diverting energy to maintain a particular area, the imbalance becomes aggravated because you have a destructive energy field generated by the condition, surrounded and interpenetrated by the energy your body is supplying to the area to correct the condition. If you're trying to generate an energy flow around and through yourself to do some form of magickal work, there's an area of interference that has to be overcome and, obviously, that means it's going to take more energy to compensate for that. It's a situation that's going to make things harder for you any way you look at it. Get your body into a healthy state and keep it that way. If you can do that, you will have more energy to expend on your work with less internal interference.

What's it going to take to do this? The stock answers are the good answers.

Diet and Exercise

Start with the diet. I have a friend with two young children who has a rare attitude about meals. (1) Prepare a healthy, balanced meal; (2) put it in front of the children; (3) leave them alone. Sometimes they eat everything; sometimes they eat virtually nothing. But they're never forced to eat anything or everything. The result is sometimes rather strange to observe. They devour french fries, of course, like most children do, but chicken and seafood are also high on their lists. Often they won't touch a salad, but other times they like to munch on raw carrots, celery, broccoli, cauliflower and other vegetables if these are put out for them as snacks. Oranges and bananas go quickly. On the other hand, sometimes they won't eat a thing on their plates, but as soon as the table is cleared they'll make peanut butter sandwiches for themselves.

The point is, when we're young there seems to be much better communication between body and mind. When the body needs something in particular, it lets us know and we instinctively go after the appropriate foods. As adults we have a tendency to forget that. So first off, just listen to your own body. When you're hungry, instead of concentrating on what will be quickest and easiest to fix, run down a mental list of possible foods and see what sounds best to your body. Then accommodate it. If your body says it needs a pepperoni pizza, that's okay. Maybe your body needs something from the cheese.

That's the easiest and most natural way. For those of you who prefer (or require) something a little more regimented, by all means read up on nutrition. Find out what foods provide nutrients the body needs and get them. This is especially important if you're trying to listen to your body and all it seems to be doing is growling at you.

The basic, general rules are really very simple. First, go after green, leafy vegetables—lettuce, spinach and the like. Actually, any vegetable at all is probably going to be good for you, preferably raw, or cooked as little as possible. (In most cases, once something is cooked to the point of being soft you've cooked away most of what you're eating it for to begin with.) Fruits and nuts are good, too. Chicken and seafood are infinitely better than steak. (Aside from all the chemicals that are fed or injected into cattle, everything you eat retains some of the energy of its source. The higher the animal, the more energy it retains, and that energy can interfere with your own.)

Another important aspect is to eat when you're hungry, and don't eat when you're not hungry. Again, *listen* to your body. You are not under any social requirement that demands you eat breakfast when you get up, lunch at noon and dinner in the evening. Eat when your body tells you it needs something.

Give it what it needs, when it needs it, as often as it needs it, but no more. It could be, for instance, that if you take a sandwich to work and eat part of it in the morning and part in the afternoon instead of the whole thing during "lunchtime," you'll feel better. Or maybe you should bring a stash of apples or carrot sticks or some other fruits or vegetables with you and just nibble on them throughout the day. Two or three snacks after you get home may prove better for you than one big sit-down meal.

Experiment. Forget about routine and the expectations of others. There are no hard-and-fast rules, just listen and trust your body to let you know what's best for you. On the other hand, if you aren't sure what your body is saying, follow the guidelines above, and try going to a health food store or a New Age bookstore for a book on nutrition. (It never hurts to understand *why* your body's asking for a particular food.)

For those of you who are a little (or a lot) overweight, a couple of words about dieting: do it. But keep in mind that your stomach is going to ask for a lot more than your body really needs, though your body will need more than it would if you were a hundred pounds lighter. If you feel like you've got to go on a crash diet, go ahead. It's not the healthiest thing to do, but as individuals, we do what we must. Sometimes your body will let you know that it needs something in particular and you'll be better off providing that food than you would be in thinking only about avoiding the calories. Your body doesn't want to be sick, so combine a good ear with common sense—meaning peanut butter (protein) may be okay, but if you think you're hearing "chocolate fudge layer cake a la mode," double check where that voice is coming from.

Fasting has its place, too, for cleaning out the system in general and opening up psychic channels. It's also been known to result in outright hallucinations, along with other things such as kidney damage, liver damage, eye damage, etc. As a short-term way of cleaning yourself out, it's fine; as a way of losing weight, I wouldn't recommend it. Besides, it likely will leave you feeling very weak and tired, and that isn't healthy if you have to hold down a job. Try to be practical about it.

The matter of diet is one of the easiest to handle, but other elements of the physical side of personal power also need to be addressed. One is breathing and another is exercise. I'm going to skim over these, not because they're not important, but rather because they're too complex to cover respectably here.

Breathing is important, and not just because we'd be in some trouble if we stopped. In India, for instance, breathing has evolved into a science. Whether it developed by means of experimentation, intuition or guidance from beings on higher planes, I'm not in a position to judge. Disciplined breathing exercises such as you'll find in many books on yoga will help you for a number of reasons. Proper breathing helps to balance the energies inside you and to stimulate certain energy centers. It also enables you to draw in more energy and to dispel more of the toxins already accumulated in your body. Increased discipline also comes with controlled breathing. Study it. It will help.

Exercise, like proper eating, helps to increase balance and purify the body. If you want to try yoga exercises, that's fine; if you prefer running around the block a few times or doing aerobics at home with a video tape for company, then go for it. Whatever you do to help maintain the body in good, healthy condition will go a long way toward facilitating your attempts at magick later on.

Now, this talk about maintaining a healthy diet, exercising, and breathing right is all good and well, but let's be realistic. Like many of you, I live in a big city, hold a full-time job, and know just how hard self-discipline can be. During that commute home after a trying day at work those fast-food places start looking awfully inviting! Aside from that, I'll also admit to having a couple of cups of coffee in the morning and keeping a package of chocolate cookies in my desk for when I'm working late. As nice as it might be, I don't anticipate reaching perfection in this particular lifetime.

Let me tell you a short story. Some years back I was invited to a Buddhist retreat to hear an address by the Dalai Lama during one of his visits to the United States. (The Dalai Lama is the spiritual leader of the Buddhists, the former political ruler of Tibet who was deposed by the Chinese, and a recent recipient of the Nobel Peace Prize. He is considered to be a Perfect Master. He's very quiet, and very impressive.) As could well be expected, someone asked him how it's possible to live a spiritual life, striving for perfection, while living in our materialistic world with the demands and responsibilities it places on us. His answer was rather simple in its recognition of our reality: don't expect to reach perfection all at once, or even in this lifetime. It's something you work toward. If you spend half your time on the needs of this life and half your time on matters pertaining to your spiritual future, eventually you'll get there.

What I'm attempting to communicate is the ideal. If you eat right, exercise right, meditate right, breathe right, etc., it'll be much easier to generate the maximum amount of energy your body is capable of, to draw in more energy when you need it, and to summon whatever additional help you need. The body is a marvelous mechanism. A Big Mac isn't going to kill you. A big party isn't going to leave you magickally incompetent, either. (Well, not for too long, anyway.) You can live a fairly normal life and still be effective, as long as you don't overindulge and recognize that you're going to have to put some time into recharging yourself before you do any work. Your mind and body may both become so accustomed to doing the "right" thing that temptations will be few and far between, and easily resisted. But it's all right to work up to that.

Mental Energy, Meditation and Visualization

For the magician/witch, all magick starts, and too frequently ends, in the mind. You can't do a thing without it. Disciplining the body is one thing, but disciplining the mind is something else entirely. I'm talking discipline here, not intelligence. Discipline and intelligence are very different things. Some brilliant, inventive minds have had little discipline, floating from one thought to another so quickly that nothing ever came of any idea they ever had (unless it was passed on to someone else). On the other hand, people with average or even below-average intelligence are capable of developing mental discipline.

Some degree of mental discipline will develop naturally out of your efforts toward physical discipline. The control of your diet, use of the breathing exercises, and the physical exercises, if followed religiously, will give you a certain amount of mental discipline. But there's more to it than that. You should also practice meditation.

Meditation is actually a form of self-hypnosis or auto-hypnosis. You'll be using it later in your work. Meditation will help you to center yourself. By centering I mean going into yourself and making sure everything is in balance and quiet: no turmoil, no nervous twitches, no hands shaking. Learn to relax. It relates back to what I said about how physical imbalances can interfere with the energy flow around and through your body. Tension can do the same thing. Calm down first; you can get the adrenaline flowing later when you need it. Meditation will help you do this.

Meditating also helps you to center your thoughts—to concentrate on one thing while ignoring distractions. This is a *very* big thing. When you start working it will be vital that all you think about is the end result you wish to achieve, what I call "the Desired End Result." Thinking ahead to Saturday night isn't going to do you one bit of good. In some cases allowing distractions could be outright dangerous to you.

Finally, meditation will help you with mental visualization. There are a number of steps you follow in setting up a magick ritual, some of which you'll recognize from the movies, if nothing else. You create a circle to work in, for instance. You need to be able to *see* that circle while you're creating it. The more clearly you see it in your mind, the more energy you'll put into it and the stronger it will be. The stronger the circle is, the less your energy will be dissipated wastefully into the air before you're ready.

Visualization is usually essential when you evoke assistance from other beings, whether they're elementals or deities. Combining a strong mental image with everything else will help open the lines of communication more easily.

Visualization is indispensable in realizing the goal of your work. Whatever you want to accomplish, you've got to be able to picture it in your own mind and to hold that picture through everything else you do. Every ounce of energy you can generate will be directed into that picture in your mind. If you can't hold the picture, that energy will go elsewhere and will be either dissipated, wasted, or used to do something you don't want done. That's why meditation is important. (Trust me on this one.)

So much for discipline and meditation. What about mental energy? Actually, I've just given you the most important aspects of the subject. That the brain generates energy has been proven scientifically. What hasn't been scientifically proven, but what we're going to accept on faith, is that the mind (through the brain) generates energies beyond what instruments can register. This belief is the heart of all magick. You create an image in your mind of what you want to accomplish, concentrate on it until you can almost taste it, and put every ounce of energy you can muster into bringing it to life.

The mind can do more than generate energy. It can draw in and control energy from outside of itself. The mind can tap into the universal energy around us, draw it in, concentrate it, shape it and use it. The same applies to Nature energy. Mental energy is what shapes the images we project of the Desired End Result and gives those images life on another plane so they can reflect back into our own world as reality. Mental energy also helps open the pathways of communication between us and everything that exists on other planes.

Energy and Will. That's what it's all about. Energy and Will. With your physical body in balance so there's no interference, the mind can function unfettered, mustering all the energies available from this world and others, concentrating and refocusing them to accomplish whatever you want.

Different schools have different ideas on personal power and the best way to develop it. It's good, and wise, to keep an open mind on *all* possibilities—the various options presented here and others—because different people are generally suited to different schools, different religions and different paths, with so many to choose from. Some in the Craft prefer the Celtic tradition and some feel more comfortable with the Egyptian tradition. Some prefer Wicca while others work better with ceremonial magick. Some people tend toward the activity of occultism while others are more amenable to the comparative passivity of Eastern mysticism. Just as there are the different paths to spiritual development, there are also different branches of each path, each with its own lessons and emphasis.

Another approach to personal power, for instance, is that of the sorcerer, as found in the writings of Carlos Castaneda. I recommend his works if for no other reason than to provide another perspective to the one I'm giving here. Many of his concepts are shared with European magickal traditions and many are unique to the particular path he presents. You might find the way of the sorcerer to be more in touch with your own temperament, or you may find ways of combining the knowledge gleaned from those books as well as this one and others. Start with *The Teachings of Don Juan.*[1]

Psychic Abilities

There are energies which the body itself just isn't likely to tap into without conscious effort. The psychic energies combine the mental and spiritual sides of man. The energies we use for such things as telepathy, clairvoyance, and psychokinesis (mind-over-

---

[1]Carlos Castaneda, *The Teachings of Don Juan: A Yaqui Way of Knowledge.* New York: Pocket Books, 1974. Also, *Tales of Power*, New York: Washington Square Press, 1974. (There are seven books in all by Castaneda; if you don't read them in sequence you'll easily get lost.)

matter), as well as contacting other entities, the cosmic consciousness, the akashic records, etc., are more than just energies
generated by our physical bodies or minds; they're tied in with
our spiritual nature. The mind may provide the direction, the
will, but the communication or contact is accomplished on another level.

In working magick the individual starts with emotional energy (desire) and converts it (will) into psychic energy (power).
Magick isn't merely some form of alpha waves or theta waves
created by chemical reactions in the brain or all the tests run on
psychics in laboratories for the last thirty or forty years would
have revealed more than they have.

In terms of specific psychic abilities, different people have
different areas in which they're adept. Some, for instance, are
particularly good at telepathy, but not in clairvoyance (distant
seeing), while others do better with clairsentience (distant feeling). Others can use their psychic energies to contact entities on
other planes or to "read" the akashic records (a kind of library,
containing all the history and knowledge of the universe). Some
people don't seem to be able to do any of these things, but they
still function well magickally, being able to manipulate energies
to alter their environment at will.

Most young children seem to have natural psychic abilities.
Many a so-called "invisible friend" is really a form of spirit entity
with which the child is able to communicate. Most children can
see auras. Frequently, though with occasional difficulty in making
myself understood because of vocabulary, I'll ask children if they
can see any colors around someone, with interesting results.
Try it sometime. (If you use the color associations in the
Appendices under both Planetary Correspondences and Candle
Colors, you should be able to deduce the significance of auric
colors.) If you'd like another little experiment, the next time
you're standing in a line and you see an infant who seems
bored or is just observing the world around it, try sending out
some energy in its direction in the form of a pink light and
watch the reaction you get. Most of the time it will elicit a
smile. (Pink is the color of love.)

Like all other forms of energy, the use of psychic energy can be learned. Some people maintain some of the psychic awareness they had as children. Others succeed in regaining the ability by playing related mental games such as trying to focus on someone to determine their occupation. The deliberate attempt to focus your attention on people and to tune in to them is a good way to reestablish your psychic energy.

Another game is to have someone give you something that belongs to someone else to see what you can get from it. Hold it in your hand, feel it, let your mind float and see what kind of pictures or feelings come to you. Sometimes you'll be wrong and sometimes right. When you're right, and you're satisfied your awareness is specific enough not to be coincidence, go with it and take it as further encouragement. Don't hesitate to ask for immediate feedback, especially when you're just starting out. It might help you to focus better. On the other hand, after a few negative responses it may turn out that you're tuning in to some-one else entirely and the person giving you the feedback couldn't realize that based on just a few pieces of information. It takes time and practice to become adept at using your psychic skills, but when you do, whole new worlds can open up to you. (Psychic energy is even being used now to locate archaeological sites in the U.S., Egypt and elsewhere.)

Some schools and courses can help you get started. If you're not particularly New Age oriented and don't want too much religion or philosophy, you might learn to open up at Silva Mind Control classes given from time to time in most areas. (Check the phone book covering the largest city near you for a listing.)

You might surprise yourself. With a little work and will, most people find they can function psychically in some manner. Allow yourself a little time to find your own niche. Avoid things like seances and ouija boards at the outset. They're good and valid ways of developing psychically and can provide a lot of useful information, but until you're more knowledgeable and sensitive to such things, the possibilities of being tricked, lied to or even possessed are too high to risk.

In my early days I discovered that my first working partner was subject to possession by a particular entity. It wasn't very secretive and told us its name. Discreet consultations with others turned up another woman who had experienced the same symptoms, and she even identified it by the same name! Reviewing her history, we traced the contact back a number of years to when she, her former husband and some friends spent their evenings playing with a ouija board. It took more than two months of time and effort before she was able to remain normal and free of any influence from this entity.

Don't take chances you don't have to. There are plenty of routes open for developing your psychic abilities without resorting to contacting the dead or the disembodied. Save that for later when you have more personal power, knowledge and experience so you can minimize the risks involved. Then, if you feel you need to try it, go ahead. But never, ever, under any circumstances, do it alone! Got that? Regardless of what others may tell you, ouija boards and seances are *not* games.

Why be concerned about being psychic at all? Well, psychic energy is what we actually use to work magick, but there is more. Being able to *see* psychically, whether through clairvoyance or clairsentience, will help you know when you've been successful in summoning or banishing an entity. Also, psychic ability will help you communicate with other beings who don't have physical bodies through which to talk. This skill is vital because it will help you become aware of more of the world around you—the things that exist in the world which the eyes can't detect—and it will provide a new source of additional information.

Sexual Energy

Sexual energy is more than just an aspect of physical energy. Sex can be a spiritual sharing. It's used as an invocation to a deity (asking it to enter your body). Sex can be used to perform magick or to open or close (ground) psychic channels.

Many people get involved with magick, Wicca, paganism, witchcraft, satanism, etc., thinking they will find a new source for sexual partners. If that idea's occurred to you, forget it. While most witches (both women and men) are rather open about sex, for most it's still a ritual practice. As invocation, sex is a religious practice. Likewise, used magickally, sex is not intended for physical pleasure, and having an orgasm is a means to an end and not the end itself. If you get into a group that uses sex for religious or magickal purposes and that's not what you're there for, they'll know it and probably you'll be asked to leave before long. Also, using sex for magick takes a lot of concentration and not a little bit of study. It's a lot of work and, frankly, you can get your fun a lot more easily somewhere else. This isn't the place for you.

Sexual stimulation generates a lot of energy, most of which is released very quickly in one burst at the time of orgasm. Usually the energy just goes off into space. Some of it may go to your partner, depending on what you're thinking about at the time. When used for magickal purposes, that energy is not allowed to dissipate itself freely into the atmosphere, but rather is harnessed and directed by conscious effort into a mental image of a Desired End Result. It can be fast and effective for some work, especially work of a sexual and/or emotional nature, but it's not as easy as it may sound.

Successful magick requires concentration and strong visualization. While visualization (e.g., mentally fantasizing about a partner) may be a common aspect of sexual play for most people, concentration usually loses something along the way. Holding a mental picture clearly in the mind while your body is doing its own thing is a little difficult. Actually, it's close to impossible. Most of us think of good sex as a means of letting go, and/or as requiring a letting go, of consciousness and control. We anticipate it; we expect it; we look forward to it. *Not* letting go and deliberately keeping control, which is required in much of magick, is inamicable to this approach, but so it goes. Once more it's a matter of discipline, and once more it's something you're going to have to work on and learn to control if you have any intention of availing yourself of this form of power.

Various theories exist about why intercourse seems to open the psychic channels in a person. The important thing is that it happens, especially for women.

Some people tend to see past lives. In the relaxing moments immediately following orgasm, you may be able to see your partner's face changing into what that person looked like years or millennia ago, or you may even see or somehow sense your own past. If you go with it, you may find yourself seeing, hearing or feeling things associated with a previous life.

One woman I know seems immediately to tune in to what is probably the akashic records when sex has been particularly good. She'll lie back and announce, "You may now ask me whatever you wish." Past lives, present relationships and elements of the future all seem to be fair game at this point and the information received during these times generally seems reliable (when it can be verified through research or time).

I'd like to touch on two other aspects of sex which, while not exactly related to magick, are related to energy and power. For one thing, sexual stimulation creates a condition of suggestibility. As evidence, most people I know have found themselves doing things when stimulated which they never thought of or believed they would do. Verbalizing your desires or thoughts in the form of suggestions or commands while sexually stimulating your partner can often produce interesting effects. If you've been having trouble accomplishing something because of an energy block or mental block of some kind, this is where it more easily can be removed. Also, by implication, it can be used to deliberately open specific centers of psychic functioning. In this manner it becomes possible, for instance, for one partner to direct the other to tune in to someone, someplace or something for gathering information.

Finally, remember that in the end everything comes down to a matter of energy. In using sex for magickal work, you want to generate energy which can be directed to your Desired End Result. Creating a *flow* of energy between you and your partner is vital for this. If you can visualize a circuit from you, into your partner, then back again, the energy can be put into motion, built up, and even augmented from outside. The input and output points can be whatever you'd like, but usually will come to you intuitively and spontaneously. The eyes, mouth, hands, chest (heart chakra), solar plexus, and genital area are all natural, common points for the energy to flow between partners. Also, if you take some time to explore and experiment with each other you should become aware of many other points on the body, front and back, which are energy centers you can utilize. Deliberately stimulating these points by visualizing energy flowing from your hands (for instance) into them can be helpful when you're trying to do some work.

Still, energy doesn't necessarily have to flow in a complete circuit between two people. It can be input through sensitive areas by one person, as I mentioned, or it can just as easily be pulled out and absorbed. You can use this as a method of recharging someone who's feeling drained ("the laying on of hands") or to help "drain" someone who's feeling especially hyper.

These are the positive applications of a one-way energy flow, and are presumed to involve voluntary cooperation; they can as easily be applied in a negative manner, with involuntary cooperation or without the other person's knowledge, as I'll get into shortly.

So sex is powerful, both as a magickal tool and as an opener of psychic channels. If you want more information on this subject, a number of books are available on both Western approaches to sex magick and the Eastern teachings of Tantra and Tantric sex.

You have a lot of energy inside you if you work at developing it. You can (and should) avail yourself of personal, physical power, kundalini, psychic power and sexual power. Every little bit helps, and if you can successfully develop your potential in all of these areas, you're going to be well on your way to becoming a successful worker of magick.

Earth Power

Let's start with some scientifically established facts. First, the earth is surrounded by a magnetic field that is measurable and that fluctuates. Second, the ground itself has a detectable magnetic field which measures from 0.30 of a gauss to 0.70, though this can vary depending on the composition of the ground at any given point. Third, humans also emit a measurable electric field. Fourth, motion of one medium or field through another creates an intensification of that field.

Everything alive produces energy. Whether from digesting food or photosynthesis, a constant conversion of matter from one form to another releases energy that humans can tap into. Trees, especially large ones, can be good sources of energy. If you're feeling run down, go hug a tree for awhile. It may sound silly, and you might look silly, but you can draw energy into yourself this way.

Rivers have energy, too. The motion of the water flowing sets up an energy field that you can sometimes feel if you relax and open yourself to it. Storms have power, too, whether they're wind storms, thunderstorms, tornadoes or hurricanes. Energy must be generated and dissipated for a wind to blow or a storm to rage, and you can avail yourself of that energy. Those of an adventurous nature who have stood on top of a hill facing into a driving rain with lightning flashing all around know something of just how much power can be found under such circumstances. (I officially abstain from endorsing such dangerous behavior, so if you actually try this and get burned, don't blame me!)

The earth itself has a great deal of power, too. With its molten mass of matter flowing around inside and the continents drifting around on its surface. Some places seem to have more power than others. Mountain peaks are almost invariably centers of power. Most people throughout history who have been close to the land have known of these places and have utilized them in some manner. In Britain, for instance, these were the sites of pagan rituals; most eventually were expropriated by the missionaries of Rome for churches. Many others, such as Stonehenge, are still marked by standing stones. It has been theorized that the early English built their villages on hilltops because of the power in these locations and not merely for defensive purposes. For native North Americans—in Canada, the U.S. and Mexico—these energy centers became ceremonial sites and holy ground.

Like a connect-the-dots game, these power places are joined by lines of power. Generally called ley lines (in China they're lung meis, or "dragon paths"), they're something akin to the veins in the human body, joining the entire globe into one continuous network of flowing energy. They, too, can be felt, and a popular recreation in Britain for a time was finding these ley lines, tracing them on a map and seeing what and how many points of note were on them.

Power places and ley lines have a noticeable special energy to them. Once you accept the idea that they exist and start becoming more sensitive psychically, you'll be able to identify these places for yourself. When you can feel them, you can begin pulling the energy from them and utilizing it.

There's another source of power which needs to be looked at, though it's awkward trying to qualify it as personal, psychic, or nature. Just as energy can be absorbed from plants, the earth and the rest of the world around us, it can also be obtained from animals and from other people, and this *is* a primary source for many people.

Some people tap into the life energy of other people. This process has been given the unfortunate name "psychic vampirism." In the myths, vampires supposedly sustained themselves with the blood of their victims. The psychic vampire is someone who drains you of your life energy, your vital force.

Some people do this without knowing that they do it, and some people never notice that they are being drained of their energy. There are other people who make it a regular practice to tap into an individual or a group and drain energy, which they then use for other purposes. It can often be done without anyone knowing what's happening; you can walk into a room, or talk on the phone with such a psychic vampire, and feel exhausted afterward.

A different aspect of this energy drain is involved in animal sacrifices. Supposedly, animal sacrifices release energy which magicians can then apply to their own magickal work. The truth is, using the energy of an animal sacrifice is far beyond the abilities of most magicians. This is why those who practice magic in those traditions that do use animal sacrifice rarely achieve success in their efforts. I don't advocate killing animals for any purpose except food. If you eat meat you are killing animals—however indirectly—and that is a moral issue we all have to decide for ourselves.

Some readers might condemn me for mentioning animal sacrifices, or even psychic vampirism. But if you are involved with magic in *any* form, you will eventually encounter someone or some group that practices one or the other. If you do not encounter this yourself, you'll hear about it from someone. It's a good idea to know how power can be misused, especially when you are studying how to empower yourself.

The real issue here is that you should know that these things exist. There is energy available, and it is accessible to those few advanced magicians who know how to use it. The energy can possibly be used for your own ends, so you need to be aware of its existence.

So here is the next problem to consider. Whether you are talking of feeding off the energies of another person, or absorbing energies from animal sacrifices, the form of the energy is the same. It is the energy of the life force. But is feeding moral and killing immoral? Or is feeding also immoral, but less immoral than killing? Or are they equally immoral? Or equally moral for that

matter? As in other instances, morality is always a personal determination, and it is this personal point of view that causes one
group of people to label another group of people as immoral or as
members of some crazy cult. In the middle of it all, you have to
be aware of the choices presented to you, the risks you incur, and
the potential dangers you face.

CHAPTER THREE

Paganism and Mythology

M OST MAGICK TRADITIONS ARE rooted in pagan
religions historically, though it's not necessary to par-
ticipate in one of them to practice magick. Most people
still associate magick with the traditional images—witches, war-
locks, demons and devils—created by the Catholic Church during the days of the Inquisition. So let's set the record straight on
the "Craft."

Paganism is a nature-oriented religion involving the recognition of the feminine-masculine principle in creation with a goddess who represents the female, positive, creative aspect and a
god who represents the male, negative, power aspect. Everything
is believed to be a manifestation of one of these two forces:
feminine or masculine, female or male, positive or negative. (I
use the non-traditional association of female with positive and
male with negative because of allusions frequently made to electricity, where the negative terminal produces the excess of electrons and sends them to the positive pole, thus creating the
current. In magick, likewise, the male channels energy to the
female.) Usually other, lesser gods and goddesses go along with
these two, but they represent aspects of one who is above all the
others. This is part of the basis for the expression, "All gods are
one god and all goddesses are one goddess."

Pagans

So, pagans worship a goddess and god who together represent all the forces of nature and creation. The first humans may have been pagans. In A.D. 100, Philo explained that the first generations of people considered the earth and its products as gods and worshipped them. Early humans drew their life from the earth; they couldn't live without the plants, animals and water that the earth provided, nor could they live without the warmth and light of the sun, so they worshipped all aspects of creation. When a plant or animal died, they were remorseful, for it was a personal loss to them. They, too, were worshipped, that they might reproduce. Hence paganism was a fertility religion.

The word pagan today has many negative connotations, but it is innocent of most of the bad reputation it's gotten. The Romans had a word—*pagani*—which was applied to all who lived in rural areas. Pagan means, roughly, "those who live in the country." At the time of the Roman Empire, most of the people of Europe, including the Romans, had fertility religions with a god and goddess. When Rome was Christianized, people in the outlying districts retained their old beliefs, so all pagans were non-Christian.

Witches

It's said that all witches are pagans but not all pagans are witches. This is true if one accepts the premise that a witch is a person who has undergone formal initiation into the Craft. However, if you take the term witch in the traditional sense—meaning one who practices "the craft of the wise," magick—then it's not true, for many non-pagans are and have been witches. By this standard, some Christian saints must be considered witches. Indeed, many saints were actually pagan gods adopted by the church because the strength of belief held by their followers could not be ignored.

Generally, witches are individuals who have learned how to influence the forces and energies of nature. This influence may be used either to cause or prevent events. For instance, a witch might cause a field or flock to be especially fertile or might stop a storm from releasing its rain over a town during a festival (or flood). Magick of this sort might be attempted through direct intervention by the witch with the use of the witch's own power, or through the intervention of the witch's goddess.

The system of beliefs of witches, and the source of the word itself, is Wicca. This traces back to Old English in which the word for a wise man was "wicca," a wise woman was a "wicce" and wise people were called "wiccan." In Middle English the masculine and feminine forms were combined and the new word became "wicche." It was a small step from wicche to witch. A witch, therefore, is a person who is wise in the ways of nature. By extension, witchcraft is the craft of the wise.

Wicca doesn't exist simply to worship two beings as goddess and god, nor to learn magick. It's meant to teach the nature of the forces and energies around us. After you learn this you may be able to control these forces, and that makes for the magick. With such knowledge, as well as understanding and common sense, you can gain wisdom. The central aim of Wicca is the spiritual and psychic development of each individual, and that's just another path towards the same goal most religions share.

Traditions

Wicca, or witchcraft, includes the practice of magick and uses prayers to the goddess, god and/or the witch's own personal power. A person is not officially recognized as a witch without having undergone initiation into the Craft. The term tradition is used to designate a heritage of religion and magick handed down through the years, as were the various mystery schools of Egypt, Greece, Rome and other societies. These teachings included an understanding of the nature of humankind, the world and all creation as well as the powers at work in the world. Students were taught how to use their minds to harness these powers to accomplish particular ends, so each of the old religions included a system of magick. In the old mystery schools teaching was done by word of mouth, handed down from priest to initiate. In the last few hundred years, initiates have kept the teachings in a hand-written book. This "Book of Shadows" includes the rituals, prayers, incantations and various other information used in the practice of magick and frequently also includes a history of the group itself. This use of the Book of Shadows as the personal record for each individual is still in practice today.

There are various traditions of Wicca in the world today that we will consider later. Suffice it to say that they all practice magick and hold in common a belief in a goddess and a god.

Witchcraft was never stamped out by the Church. It was forced to go underground, but it survived and today it's growing in popularity again. The modern resurgence of witchcraft is traced by many to Gerald Gardner,[2] an initiated witch who broke with tradition and publicly proclaimed himself to be a witch, writing a number of books on the subject. He was praised for this by many who felt people of today have a need for this knowledge and for an option to the popular religions which many feel offer them nothing. Others, of course, condemned Gardner for his actions in breaking vows of secrecy and risking a return to "the Burning Times." It was through Gardner's work that the popular revival of Wicca began and has spread to the extent it has. Those who follow the teachings of the Craft as passed on by Gardner are called Gardnerians and are perhaps the largest tradition of the Craft found today.

One reason paganism has become popular in the modern world is that it is considered a happy religion. It's not composed of a long list of don'ts and sins and evils designed to create guilt. "Do what you will but harm none shall be the whole of the Law. Love is the Law, Love under Will." In other words, try to love everyone and do anything you want as long as you don't hurt

---

[2]See the Bibliography for works by Gerald Gardner.

anyone in the process without their full knowledge and willing cooperation. The freedom and celebration of life encouraged by paganism has generally been in conflict with the Church, but today people feel freer to think and do as they desire and don't accept that anything that brings pleasure is, by definition, evil and sinful.

Virtually every religion in the world today is polytheistic, though in some cases this is disguised through the selective use of terminology. God the Father and God the Son are still two. Catholics have Father, Son and Holy Ghost, along with Mary and a host of saints whom they can invoke. Officially these saints and angels are only to be intermediaries, but in practice many people pray *to* them for *direct* intervention, as in "Saint Christopher protect us on this journey," and not "Saint Christopher, please ask God to protect us on this journey." Since some Catholic saints were pagan gods and goddesses appropriated by the church to ease the conversion process, it can be argued that Catholics often invoke pagan deities.[3]

Pagan goddesses have had many different names in different civilizations throughout history. For example, Aphrodite (Rome), is also known as Arianrhod (British Isles), Artemis, Asherat, Ashtar (Phoenicia), Astarte, Athene (Greece), Ba'alat (Byblos), Bride, Brigid, Ceres, Danu (Ireland), Demeter, Diana, Dionë, Cerridwyn, Freya (Saxon), Frig (Norse), Gaea, Hathor, Hecate (Thrace), Ishtar (Babylon), Isis, Kore, Melusine, Persephone, Rhea, Tailltiu, Tanit (Carthage), Tlazolteotl (Aztec), and many more. What most of these share in common is that they were associated with the moon and fertility, and many were pictured carrying a bow.

---

[3]The Catholic missionaries, when faced with opposition to change by the natives, frequently "adopted" the local deities as saints and built churches on holy spots as a means of getting the locals into church. The correspondences between Catholicism and paganism and other religions appears in many sources, but if you want a good book on the history, see *Pagan Celtic Britain* by Ann Ross, published by Sphere Books, London, 1974.

The god, too, is represented by many names, like Amon, Cernunnos, Dionysus, Donar, Goidelic, Gwydion, Jupiter, Math Van Mathonwy, Mithra, Odin, Pan, Pasupati, Perkunas, Perun, Ra, Taara, Taranis, Thunar, Tugh, Woden, Zeus, etc. He was usually pictured with horns, associated with animals and the sun. While the goddess usually rules the moon and life and fertility, the god rules the sun, the land of the dead and hunting.

The pagans of today do not believe in an actual goddess and god as co-creators of the world, nor do they believe that the sun and moon are deities. The goddess and god represent the creative forces in the universe—the duality of nature. It's much easier to picture two human-like figures than it is to imagine an amorphous creative energy force. Most Catholic churches have representations of Jesus on a cross, but followers don't believe the representation itself is Jesus. The symbol helps them to attune to the Christ spirit. Likewise, the statues of the goddess and god found on pagan altars are not idols worshipped as realities, but represent in human form the abstract principles of creation. The concepts of the goddess and god have been worshipped for centuries, and today's pagans can still salute the old gods, call on them, and utilize them without accepting them as the ultimate creators of the universe.

Most societies have developed lore to explain where their deities came from, what they do and how the world was created. In addition to the standard mythologies of Egypt and Greece with which most people are familiar, there is a book called *Aradia: The Gospel of the Witches* by Charles Godfrey Leland.[4] Leland claims to have obtained the material for this book from an Italian witch. He refers to the goddess by her Roman name, Diana, and her brother is Lucifer. Lucifer was the Bringer of Light and was an important god in Rome until he was designated as "Satan" by the Catholic Church. He was never considered evil by pagans. (The witch trials tell of the Devil having three horns, one of which

---

[4]Charles Godfrey Leland, *Aradia: The Gospel of the Witches* (London: C.W. Daniel, 1974).

was a light, which serves to demonstrate the concept of the horned god as the bringer of light. Light is known to be used even today as a symbol for knowledge and wisdom.)

The legend given in *Aradia* describes Diana as the first darkness who divided herself into light as Lucifer, her brother and son. She fell in love with his light, eventually seduced him, and Aradia was born. Diana and Lucifer both came to earth and Diana taught magic and sorcery to the spirits on earth, created the heavens, the stars and rain, and later controlled the destiny of humanity. After Aradia was grown, Diana gave her responsibility for teaching humans witchcraft; Aradia also taught methods of worship of her mother, how to organize covens, conduct the ceremonies and how to pray for guidance, assistance and protection when needed.

This is an example of legends and their similarities. For instance, the first-created is nearly always a female. This is natural enough since man saw that all life came forth through the female; it logically followed that the female came before the male. This is also the reason pagans usually place the goddess slightly above the god. The extent of the separation of the two varies from tradition to tradition. Another aspect of many mythologies is the idea of the brother-husband relationship between two deities. In Greece, for instance, Gaea, the first goddess to come out of Chaos, gave birth to Uranus and had many children by him, including the 12 Titans who invented the arts and magick. Two of the offspring, Cronus and Rhea, also married, and two of their children—Zeus and Hera—did likewise.

The Evolution of Pantheons

A common concept in most myths is the idea of darkness coming first and separating itself into darkness and light. Paganism is the oldest of religions and the similarity between these stories and the one found in Genesis is hardly coincidental.

One of the biggest problems in dealing with the deities of various ancient civilizations is that of overlapping, merging, borrowing and general flux in the names and attributes of the various gods and goddesses. There's an additional hazard in identifying a given deity with a specific country. For example, a being from another world might consider earthlings to be polytheistic, believing in a pantheon of gods headed up by deities called Jesus, Allah, Jehovah, Shiva, etc. Likewise, the history of Palestine would show its inhabitants repeatedly changed their god in spite of the fact that we realize the change in deities was a matter of a change in inhabitants through immigration and conquest and not vacillation and indecision on the part of a single group.

If the pantheon of Egypt seems confused and illogical, it's probably because various gods and goddesses were worshipped in individual towns and cities at first, and as these cities grew in stature their patrons did likewise. Also, as Egypt was influenced by other cultures, Egyptian gods and goddesses merged with those of other lands with a resulting change in attributes and, in some cases, names. The same situation is found in Greece where various tribes brought their own particular deities into areas they settled or conquered where other gods were already being worshipped. Often the result was that a god of one people would become the husband of the goddess of the conquered, or the newly introduced gods would be called the fathers of the native gods.

To add to the confusion, there was a tendency to take a god or goddess with a wide range of authority and create a son or daughter to assume some of those duties. An example of this might be Demeter from Greece, who was goddess of the fields and harvest along with the Underworld. She had a daughter, Kore (Persephone), who became the bride of Hades and assumed her mother's role as goddess of the Underworld with her husband. Egypt had a sun god as well as gods associated with the rising sun, the sun at midday, and the setting sun. The result is four solar deities, all with different names.

In any event, all of these gods grew out of the amalgamation of a number of separate local cults representing various powers of growth or other factors thought beneficent to humankind. Let's look at a couple of heavenly dynasties as illustrations of how they evolved, merged and related to others.

Assyro-Babylonian Tradition

In Assyro-Babylonian tradition, the first created was Apsu, the primordial ocean. With Apsu was Tiamat, the tumultuous sea. Then came Mummu, followed by Lakhmu and Lakhaum, who were serpents. These two gave birth to Anshar and Kishar, who in turn bore the other gods. (Note the brother-sister marriages.)

Apsu, according to the myth, complained of having no peace and decided to destroy all she had created. Ea discovered the plan and through the use of magick seized Apsu and Mummu. Tiamat then declared war on Ea and a series of battles ensued. In the end, the god Marduk emerged as the leader of the forces aligned with Ea and defeated Tiamat, saving the world. In return, the gods abided by their pledge to make Marduk their king. Marduk considered it his responsibility to organize the universe and began by assigning three deities to rule the three areas of creation. To Anu went the sky, to Enlil went the earth and Ea received the waters. This is similar to the apportionment made by Zeus after his defeat of Cronus, in which Zeus retained the sky, his brother Poseidon received the waters and brother Hades was given the rule of the underworld.

Marduk became supreme among the gods by virtue of his strength and courage in battle. After organizing the universe, he created humanity. As their creator it followed that Marduk would rule those things that humans required. Hence, he was considered an agricultural deity who made the plants grow and also was the great healer and chief magician.

The chief goddess of this time was Ishtar, the daughter of Anu of the sky, sometimes thought to be the daughter of the god Sin. Ishtar was the goddess of the morn and the evening, which shows her connection with Anu. She was most popular for her attributes as Anu's daughter: she was the goddess of love and voluptuousness, and her holy city was Erech, "town of the sacred courtesans." Ishtar was credited with having taken to bed all of the other gods, along with a sizable number of different animals. As Sin's daughter she was "Lady of Battles" and took part in battles, riding a chariot with a bow in her hand.

Egypt

Egypt presents its own problems for us today. Four common systems of belief concerning the creation of the world came from the cities of Hermopolis, Heliopolis, Memphis and Busiris, and were centered around the chief deity presiding in each city. The best known of these four is the Ennead of Heliopolis, which tells of the family of Ousir, whom the Greeks called Osiris. (Many Egyptian gods are known by their Greek names, just as many Greek gods are known by their Roman names.)

Even a god needs a parent, and in this case the parent is Num, the primordial ocean. Num was a nothingness that contained everything, including Atum, which was the spirit that contained everything. Atum decided to leave Num and emerged as Atum-Ra, who then became both Atum and Ra. Now Ra could manifest as a parent, yielding Shu and Tefnut, who begat Get and Nut, who begat Osiris and Isis and Set and Nephythys in their turn. That makes four generations with Ra as the leader, ruler of all the gods, and the three generations after him becoming known as the Ennead of Heliopolis.

While most schoolchildren are told that the pharaohs of Egypt were considered to be gods, they are seldom told the legends that the first gods were thought to have ruled the country in the beginning. Egyptian history isn't just a matter of pharaohs who became gods, but includes the original gods who became the earliest pharaohs. The first Divine King of Egypt was Ra, a sun-god. We really don't know whether Ra was conceived of as a deity and then credited with being the first pharaoh or whether he was a man who became pharaoh and was deified. It's probable that some of the pharaohs were magicians of a high order, which would explain not only their deification, but also the miracles attributed to them.

Greek mythology is filled with humans who became gods. Most of the ancient gods probably were humans who, because of their courage, strength, wisdom, or some other aspect of greatness, were later thought of as deities. Considering that all of the ancient gods and goddesses exhibited human characteristics such as jealousy, pride, hate, love, and greed, this doesn't seem to be unreasonable. Egyptian gods, however, often are pictured as only partially human in form, but they were usually given the head of an animal associated with the same objects or attributes as the god.

This digression has a bearing upon the succession of divine pharaohs in Egypt. Allegedly, one god followed another as pharaoh because of old age or retirement. Ra, for instance, grew old just as any man did, and with old age came senility. Though senile, he was not an invalid, so when men plotted to overthrow him he proceeded to destroy the guilty. With this work done he then left the world.

The city of Thebes was rather powerful and its local deity became the successor to Ra. Wearing the horns of the Theban ram, Amon became the supreme god. Because of his closeness and similar attributes to Ra, Amon was later joined to Ra and given the name Amon-Ra. Amon was king of the gods and the patron of the most powerful pharaohs. As the chief he's compared to Zeus. While Ra was a solar deity first and foremost, Amon ruled over other aspects of life associated with the sun, coming to represent the forces of generation and reproduction and becoming a god of fertility. As the pharaohs came to be treated as living gods themselves, their association with Amon (Amon-Ra) gave them the immediate, earthly responsibility for the fertility of the Egyptians' fields.

Amon, in turn, gave way to Osiris, the greatest of all the horned gods of Egypt. It was the crown of Osiris after which the later human pharaohs patterned their crowns, showing they were, indeed, gods and givers of fertility. As one of the last of the god-pharaohs, Osiris brought peace and civilization to Egypt, conquered all of Asia, abolished cannibalism, taught his people how to make farming implements for raising grain and grapes, built the first temples to the gods, and instituted religious practices.

Osiris became associated with the underworld, and his legend is considered symbolic of the belief in reincarnation. After his resurrection with the help of his sister-queen Isis, he became immortal, retired, and left the rule of earth to his son Horus, and then to Thoth, who ruled for 3,226 years. Thoth (Djehuti or Zehuti), who's compared to Hermes and Hermes Trismegistus, is credited with inventing all the arts and sciences, including soothsaying, magick and medicine. He also invented writing so his teachings would not be forgotten.

Isis, Osiris's sister and queen, was a goddess associated with a town near Thebes. They were both children of Nut, the goddess of the sky, who is associated with the Greek Rhea. Isis eventually absorbed all of the other goddesses and was credited with teaching how to grind corn, spin flax, weave cloth and cure disease. She also instituted the practice of marriage as her contribution to her husband's work of bringing peace and domesticating humanity. Isis was a great magician, also, and is frequently called upon by today's witches.

You've seen how one god or goddess could become another; let's now follow some trails.

There was a goddess named Asherat-of-the-Sea who evolved into Ashtart, later Astarte. Then there was Lilith (first found in a terra-cotta relief dating back to 2,000 B.C.), who, as a moon goddess, seductress and hunter, was associated with the Greek Diana. Lilith became Belili, then Belial, who became combined with Ishtar. Ishtar became equated with Astarte, too, thus equating Astarte and Diana. A Phoenician goddess worked her way through Cythero and Cypress to Greece, where she became Aphrodite, who shared attributes with Demeter, Hera and Selene and was equated with Isis. Diana was also sometimes equated with Aphrodite and Isis, and also has her counterparts in other parts of Europe through the ages, as covered in part by the listing at the beginning of this chapter. Got all that?

On the male side were Enlil and Marduk, mentioned earlier, who later became Bel. Enlil was also equated with Zeus, thereby equating Bel with Zeus, who was also equated with Ra, who was the successor to Amon who, as a sun god, also was compared to the Persian Mithra. Aristaeus of Thessaly was the same as Mysia's Priapus who equated with Pan and Dionysus, who were compared with Cernunnos of the Celts, Jauna or Janicot of the Basques, and Herne and Neck and Nick (who later became St. Nicholas). Cernunnos is also similar to Gwydion, who became the Welsh Math Vab Mathonwy, who is equated to Ireland's Goidelic.

You may now tear up your scorecards.

The reason for this rather lengthy section on paganism and various ancient religions is that, ultimately, there are two separate but related directions—two schools or levels—from which you can choose how you're going to work. One is Wicca, which is connected to paganism; the other is ceremonial or high magick.

Wicca is directly related to paganism and involves much of what is generally associated with witchcraft: the circle of people dancing, chanting and carrying knives (athames), the altar, etc. Wicca utilizes the pagan deities as a means of obtaining energy to work or to intervene on behalf of the witch, which brings in the religious element. The spirits and energies of nature are also utilized in Wicca.

Under the broad headings of paganism and Wicca, innumerable subheadings represent different traditions, such as subheadings for Egyptian, Greek or Celtic (among others), then sub-subheadings under those. For instance, the Gardnerian tradition was established by Gerald Gardner in England. There is also Alexandrianism founded by Alex Sanders, who branched off from Gardner; and Ray Buckland's "Seax Wicca" which broke away to follow the Saxon path. Feminist-oriented Dianic traditions abound as well. As you see, you can choose from plenty of traditions if you care to pick a pagan path.

Ceremonial magick is somewhat different. While Wicca usually involves a group working together, ceremonial magick is usually solo work. Wicca centers on a goddess and god of nature as a religious focus while most ceremonial magicians utilize the Judeo-Christian system of different names for God (believing that words have a power all their own), as well as the hierarchy of archangels, angels, and various other levels of spirits all the way down to the demons. These entities are not worshipped, mind you, just utilized. There are beings with power that can be used by the magician and just because a being happens to be considered an angel (or a demon), that's no reason to worship it. On the other side of the coin, the ceremonial magician is concerned only with the power attributes of an entity, not its basic nature. A ceremonial magician feels free to mobilize demonic as well as angelic forces on his behalf depending on which is more appropriate from a power point of view. (Regardless of popular tradition, associating with demons is not, of itself, evil. Demons are a category of entities with their own particular powers and abilities.) The popular image of a person in black robes standing inside a circle with a lot of designs drawn in and around it, waving a wand or sword, applies more to the ceremonial magician than it does to the Wiccan.

Wicca includes some variant of one of the pagan traditions of worship, involves a group of people, and utilizes energies generated by the group or through the individual mind (if working alone), while ceremonial magick involves ceremony and ritual, where the magician's energy is used to summon and control nonphysical entities to perform works on his behalf.

It is possible to combine these, however, since there are a number of points common to both systems. Both use circles, call on guardians to help protect the circle, use candles, incense, swords, wands, etc., organize rituals around astrological factors as well as planetary influences and attributes using principles handed down through the centuries, and depend on the power of the mind to make the magick work. Which system (or combination of systems) you choose to utilize will depend on your own temperament, your existing religious beliefs, access to other books for further information, the availability of other people to work with, and what feels most comfortable to you. Neither is right or wrong; they're different. You may want to experiment with each to determine which works best for you from both psychological and practical points of view.

Picking a Pagan Tradition

Let's take a closer look at the question of picking a pagan tradition in which to work. As convoluted as the earlier information on mythology may have sounded, there was a reason for having listed all those names (and many more could have been added!). First, you're encouraged to pick one deity, learn the tradition and rituals behind it, and use it. Second, which one you choose matters little because they're all connected to some degree with one another.

Why pick one? ". . . a lot of people have put a lot of energy into prayers, rites, rituals and sacrifices directed at these gods and goddesses." Why doesn't it matter which one you pick? Because "it's all in your mind."

Through the centuries these deities have existed on another plane. Whether that plane is above, below, beyond, beside, within or without our own doesn't really matter. They exist with all the attributes traditionally ascribed to them. The paths used to reach them are well-worn and the easiest (though not necessarily the only) way to access them is the way that's been most used in the past. Once you reach them you can draw on all the energy that's been put into them through all of time.

Pick whatever you're comfortable with. Maybe the massive, rock-hewn strength of the Assyrian or Babylonian images with the winged bull appeal to you. The image of Ishtar is probably one of the strongest of the goddesses, combining love, sex and war all in one. Or you might prefer the Egyptian with its pomp and regal regalia of gold and lapis lazuli. Maybe the Greek, Roman or Persian would appeal more to your senses. Or you might choose the simplicity and down-to-earth quality of one of the various Celtic traditions. Each has its horned god and its goddess of the moon.

Whatever image you choose should appeal to some aspect of yourself so you can relate to it in some way. In the range from the Egyptian to the Assyrian and the Celtic you should find an atmosphere that feels right. It might be necessary to try a few before you find the best one for you, but that's okay.

The reason you pick a tradition in which to work is to take advantage of what others have done in the past. The well-trod path is the easiest to follow. Which path you choose matters only to the extent that you feel comfortable with it. If you're uncomfortable calling on Ishtar, for instance, nothing is going to work for you. It also matters because of just how well the path has been trodden. For example, there's a well-used path to Diana, but a lesser-used path exists to Tanit, which can be used, but not as easily or productively. Fewer people worshipped Tanit than Diana, so there's less energy available on the path to Tanit. On the other hand, if you feel more comfortable with Tanit than Diana, that could help compensate for the energy shortage, since what's there could be more easily accessed.

Imagine a ball of light as the original, creative force. Circling this ball of light are dozens of other balls—large and small—each on its own ring circling the center ball, which are all the goddesses ever worshipped. Some have more of a charge than others, but they're all moving around the same center. Now, imagine that the circling rings have links between them so you can move from one to another, and many of these links fall close to the balls moving on each ring. For instance, Diana is moving on one ring and Aphrodite is on another, but both rings and the goddesses are so close to each other that in reaching one you are in very close proximity to the other. Diana is also linked to Ashtart, but Ashtart is closer to Astarte than Diana is. When you reach one you reach all to some degree.

The concept of the moon goddess of fertility brings you into step with a lot of different goddesses all at once, regardless of what name you use. This connection makes it possible to draw on many sources of energy at once even though you're concentrating on one in particular. This doesn't mean you get a free ride around the entire merry-go-round of deities from all of history. Some are linked more closely than others, while the ties between others are remote. Some merging of powers and influence occurs. The more widespread the worship of a particular entity and/or the more closely it is related to others, the more energy you can borrow second-hand.

Remember what was said about travelling the same path as was used in the past and take into account that each one has its own peculiarities—they are still different paths. (I'll get into more detail on that later, but suffice it to say at this point that if one person is working according to one tradition but a second person is working in a very different tradition, the first person will find it much more difficult to affect the work of the second.) The closer you adhere to the historical methods associated with a particular tradition, the easier and more effective it will be for you.

Ultimately, it's all in your mind. How easy or difficult it is to draw on that energy, or even whether you need a boost at all, depends on yourself. I'm trying to guide you into the easiest method which requires the least amount of personal energy expenditure.

CHAPTER FOUR

Other Entities

S O FAR WE'VE DISCUSSED some mythologies and part of the role deities can play in working magick. Now we're going to consider other living entities, including elementals, angels, archangels, spirits and intelligences, and familiars of different types, existing in the non-physical world around us. For some of you, the idea of working with some of these beings may be fairly easy to accept, others may find this chapter to be a strain on your credulity.

Elementals

The elementals are acknowledged and used in both the Craft and ceremonial magick. They are associated with the elements of earth, air, fire, and water. Each elemental exists wherever you find its element in any significant degree. Where there are forests, fields, mountains and valleys you'll find the elementals of earth. The elementals of air are virtually everywhere, though you might be wasting your time looking for them around sources of pollution like oil refineries. A good fire will always have them, though even a candle or match can attract the elementals of fire. The elementals of water can be found around any lake, pond, river or stream.

According to some schools of thought elementals were not created with the angels and the divine sparks that are the centers of humans. They're more like incidental results of the work that went into organizing our world. Some believe that the elementals were created by the angels, just as the various deities may have resulted from the repetition of certain human thoughts, activities and energies. Whatever the truth of their origin, that their existence is pretty well accepted is all we need be concerned with here.

Along with the basic elementals are other entities that have authority over them. (I know, I know: it's getting complicated again.) For example, according to one system the archangel of earth is Auriel; the angel is Phorlakh; the ruler is Kerub and the king is Ghob. Different systems and traditions may have different names for the king or ruler. Remember most pagan traditions don't recognize angelic entities at all. (The names associated with the other elements are listed in Appendix C.)

Earth

The elementals of earth are the most widely perceived and acknowledged around the world. In most magick traditions they're called gnomes, though this term often is used for any of the mythical little people associated with the earth, such as fairies, leprechauns, and elves. Like ghosts, gnomes are usually perceived only by their movement, detected out of the corner of your eye. If you actually see them, chances are they'll appear to be little old men, very quick on their feet. (This is a generality and not a universal truth, however.)

Gnomes have dominion over everything related to the earth—rocks and minerals or those things that grow in them. This connection with the earth led to the idea of gnomes having charge of gold. Technically that interpretation is not far off, since a cooperative elemental could be a guide to any precious metals or gems in its immediate environment.

The table of the elements and their correspondences in Appendix C indicates that gnomes are associated with the north and are generally pictured as male. Earth is firm, solid, virtually indestructible, and so it's perceived as a source of power. The principal, general-purpose banishing ritual used by ceremonial magicians, the Lesser Banishing Ritual of the Pentagram (LBR), can utilize the Earth Banishing Pentagram at all four compass points or quarterpoints, since earth is a basic source of power.

Air

The elementals of air are called sylphs. Sylphs are recalled in the present-day images of fairies. They're generally thought to be small, light, delicate creatures with wings who inhabit the air around us. With their control of the air they can be useful for influencing such things as wind, clouds and storms—or lack thereof.

Whereas the gnomes are old, the sylphs are young and quick. Also, you may remember that the words *inspiration* and *aspiration* derive from the same word as air. Therefore, the sylphs are associated with creative forces, including those that depend on imagination.

Fire

Fire, too, has its elementals, though the name and image associated with them is a little stranger than the others. These are the salamanders, and they look just like what the name implies: red salamanders. They're rarely used to cause or extinguish fires, but generally if there's a continuing flame, there will be salamanders around who can affect it.

Fire is often unpredictable, but it's also purifying and impartial, devouring nearly anything. The salamanders, then, are looked upon are being somewhat tricky and sinister, though they also represent justice.

Water

The last element is water, and the name applied to these elementals is undines, and they look like mermaids. You'll find undines around any significant body of water unless, like air, there is significant pollution. In character they're much like the sylphs— small, young and quick—but a bit heavier in nature, just as water is heavier than air.

Elementals are frequently evoked in rituals, sometimes as a courtesy and sometimes as accomplices. The guardians or rulers of the elements are usually summoned during the casting of a circle to protect it at their respective quarterpoints. When (if) you start using astrology to determine the best time to perform a certain ritual, you may decide to take advantage of certain conditions to utilize elementals to help you. For instance, if you're doing a Venus ritual and you find that the planet Venus is situated in the sign of Aquarius, then it would be to your benefit to summon the sylphs to your aid because of the relationship of sylphs to the sign of Aquarius, an air sign. Likewise for a sun ritual. The sun is associated with fire and Leo, so calling in the salamanders could be beneficial.

These are the natural elementals. There's another type of elemental that you actually create out of these elements. (See Appendix E, "Conjuration and Summoning of an Elemental.") This elemental is assembled from the four elements and is used for a particular piece of work, then disposed of as soon as that work is finished. Unlike a familiar that is maintained for as long as desired and can be used for many things, the elemental referred to here is used only once.

Angels and Archangels

Angels show up everywhere in rituals. There are angels associated with each of the elements, each planet, and each day of the week. In fact, some are angels one day and may be archangels another day. In ceremonial magick these angels, or archangels, are called upon generally to help with the work.

The word angel comes from the Greek word *angelos* and is equated with the Hebrew word *malak* which means "person sent." In other words, an angel is a sort of messenger. Archangels don't really show up much in Christian tradition in spite of the fact that they share the same Judaic roots as Christianity. Archangels do appear in other theologies and are frequently found in the Qabalah, so there's a literary basis for accepting their existence based on religious tradition. Archangel is a term of comparative rank only.

An angel is a person sent or messenger. Angels may be heavenly-created and eternal, but so are you. They're not better or higher than you, they're just different. You're capable of evolving and they're not. Angels are messengers responsible for communicating between realms and for performing specific duties assigned to them. Each has a sphere of influence and, while possessing almost unlimited influence within that sphere, can do virtually nothing for you outside of it. They are intelligent individuals with their own existence, their own minds, their own preferences, and they are entitled to due respect. (I know of someone who had difficulty with an angel who objected to the incense being used in the ritual, in spite of the fact it was technically correct. It was made clear that it would be better to burn the appropriate oil rather than the herbs, and once that change was made the matter was closed and they got along nicely.)

The names of many of these angels will be familiar to those of you who have any background at all in the Judeo-Christian tradition. The angels of the quarterpoints/elements are Auriel (earth), Raphael (air), Michael (fire) and Gabriel (water). (Angelic names generally end in the holy "el.") Raphael is also the angel associated with Mercury and Michael is its archangel; these roles are reversed for the Sun, with Michael the angel and Raphael the archangel.

Angels are summoned in ceremonial rituals to perform the work desired. As an example, if you were involved in a business deal that was being drawn out longer than you expected and you wanted to get it over with, you could turn to Appendix B and find "promptitude in business" under "On the Day" of Mercury, so on a Wednesday, the day of Mercury, you'd do a ritual calling upon Raphael to intervene on your behalf to bring negotiations to a (favorable) close.

The prevailing wisdom is that you don't use angels for negative work, but the prevailing wisdom is that you shouldn't be doing any negative work in the first place. Yet Zamael, the angel of Mars, is ostensibly called upon to sow hatred, enmity, discord and ruin, so I think there's some flexibility designed into this system.

Angels are residents of another plane that is different from ours. Their shape, form and size isn't what you're accustomed to seeing and in all likelihood you will not see them. Although you may call them to appear before you in the circle, what you perceive is an emanation of their power, not the actual entity. Hence, you can feel their presence without actually seeing them at all. Do not assume that failure to see them indicates a failure on their part to answer when you call them.

Spirits and Intelligences

Each planet has a spirit and an intelligence (except the moon, which has a "spirit of the spirits of the moon"). The intelligence of a planet is the positive side and the spirit is the negative side, and they're of a somewhat lower order than the angels. If you want to do something that requires that you use the negative aspects of a planet, utilizing the spirit of the planet is safer than resorting to a demon. The intelligence of a planet can be utilized for simpler jobs that don't require an entity on the level of importance of an angel.

You need to develop a sense about the level of importance of different beings and how that relates to the work you want to do. Archangels are above angels, and angels are above the spirits and intelligences of their respective planets as well as over their respective elementals. Generally speaking, you want to reflect objectively on how important and difficult your work is, then decide to what level of entity you want to take it. Maybe an elemental is sufficient and, if so, trying to get an archangel to do the work is simply inappropriate. You wouldn't necessarily take a job-related problem to the president of a company if a floor supervisor or foreman was capable of handling it. Likewise, you shouldn't go to an archangel with your request if the intelligence of the planet can do the job.

Demons

The opposite of an angel is a demon. I recommend you stay away from this aspect of ceremonial magick. While a demon may be a lot easier to summon than an angel, a demon is also a lot more unpredictable, undependable and independent. If you can get the cooperation of an angel, you'll get it cleanly, simply, directly and (usually) safely. With a demon you can never be sure. I've known some people who, as a sign of trust and respect, have done rituals to summon angels without doing a protective circle. Demons don't really care too much about trust and respect—they'd rather get some measure of revenge on anyone who's crazy enough to disturb them.

Also, give a demon a loophole and he'll turn it into something the size of the Grand Canyon. Even if you have a perfect protective circle, the knowledge of how to summon a demon, and the power to control him once he's summoned, you can bet he will do everything possible to assure your desire backfires one way or another. For example, if you use a demon to get money, he might find the person closest to you from whom you would inherit money and kill that person. You'd get the money you asked for, but at quite a price.

Some books can give you some good guidelines on various demons and what they'll allegedly do for you (most common, probably, Francis Barrett's *The Magus*[5]). You can find their titles and the hierarchies and principalities and seemingly endless lists of names and attributes—even drawings of their faces—but I'd still recommend that you stay clear of demonology for safety's sake. If you absolutely have to do something using the darker side, stick to using the spirits of the planets and avoid demons.

Familiars

There are two types of familiars: those that are flesh-and-blood and those that aren't. The former, mostly associated with the Craft, are more common, more believable and less useful. The latter type of familiar can be a spirit that already exists or a personal creation. The personally created familiars take a lot of time and energy to create and maintain, but they also can be much more useful.

A personal, flesh-and-blood type of familiar is an animal that's closely connected to the witch/owner to the point that a mind-link exists. This link permits the witch to go into the familiar's mind, even at a distance, and to see, hear and experience everything that the familiar does. As a simple illustration, let's say a couple of people are carrying on a conversation in another room. You can't diplomatically go in there and you can't clearly hear what's being said from a distance, but you really want to listen in. In that case, you send your familiar into the room, then tune in to its mind to see and hear everything that's happening. You can also go into the familiar's mind to tap the memories of things it's seen and heard during your absence or while it was out somewhere.

The most famous type of familiar has always been the cat. Cats are everywhere, and this makes them inconspicuous—most

[5]Francis Barrett, *The Magus* (Secaucus, NJ: The Citadel Press, 1967).

people don't pay any attention to them. If they do draw attention, it's usually to be invited inside. No one worries about talking in front of a cat. A cat is athletic, able to run quickly, follow people, jump into windows, and do it all very quietly. They also have good eyes and ears, which helps a lot when you're trying to gather information, and they're intelligent.

In theory you could use any type of animal as a familiar, but a dog, for instance, is more limited in terms of accessibility to places and drawing attention, while a bird is generally less intelligent and will usually stand out.

On another level, it's possible to project your mind/awareness into virtually any animal. Let's say, for instance, you are out in the country and get lost. Way up above you is a crow flying around. You can project yourself into that crow to see what it sees, including a way back to civilization.

Another type of familiar has its own non-physical existence but can obtain a physical one if desired. These include the types of familiar associated with the classical magicians of the Middle Ages. These familiars were spirits (or demons or some other type of entity) that magicians summoned and compelled to serve them in any way they wished. It is alleged some familiars came voluntarily to offer their services to magicians who were particularly adept in their work.

In most instances these familiars were believed to be kept in rings worn by the magician or in boxes or jars (like genies). When the familiar's assistance was needed, the magician would summon it from its temporary abode and send it out on a mission. Sometimes these familiar spirits took up residence in animals, making them somewhat similar to the first kind of elemental I mentioned, with many of the same limitations as long as it remained in that body.

Another type of non-physical familiar is the one you create yourself, that I'm going to call an artificial familiar. Creating an artificial familiar takes concentration, will power and energy, because it involves projecting an image of the familiar and pumping it up with enough energy so that it gains a kind of life of its own on another plane. In this way it's somewhat similar in principle to the gods and goddesses mentioned in the last chapter.

The advantage of having either a spirit or artificial familiar is that it has few, if any, limitations, because it doesn't have a physical body on our plane. These familiars can go through walls that would stop an animal familiar. Also, not being bound by the physical laws of our plane, the familiar can be sent anywhere in the world in the twinkling of an eye. Let's say you've got a friend in Paris you want to check up on. No problem. You send the familiar to visit your friend and it stays there until you call it back. In the meantime you go on about your regular business. Once it's back, you tune into it psychically and question it on everything it saw and heard.

The artificial familiar has many of the same advantages the spirit familiars have in terms of mobility and invisibility, with the added advantage of being personally created by and permanently linked to the magician/witch so there's no possibility of disobedience or liberation, which are risks when dealing with a spirit familiar. You can create a familiar in any shape and size that suits your fancy. However, the artificial familiar requires a lot of time and energy to create and maintain it. The energy you put into it initially will dissipate in time, so you need to continually pump more energy into it, which can be a drain. Some of these creations work actively to maintain themselves if they're ignored too long. This can also be a problem in terms of the energy drain on the creator.

I've got a personal story for you that is confessional, amusing, and cautionary.

Many years ago, before I fully appreciated what I was getting into, I thought it would be nice to create my own familiar. I have an affinity for big cats and decided I'd like having a black panther as a familiar. Picking a quiet time of night I sat down and tried to create an image of a panther in my mind and then to project that image in front of me with all the energy I could muster. The concept was sound but the execution left something to be desired: for two weeks I was followed around by a slightly mutated version of a saber-tooth tiger. (That was Lesson #1.) Each day I spent some time putting a little more energy into this image in order to strengthen it and, at the same time, worked to correct the form of the image itself.

In time there was a black panther that seemed to be about eight feet long and to weigh a few hundred pounds, though of course it actually didn't weigh anything at all. It was big, beautiful, effective, efficient, and a drain like you wouldn't believe (Lesson #2). That panther not only took all the energy I gave it, but also had a tendency to show up from time to time for feedings I wasn't expecting. The result was that I was perpetually tired, started sleeping on the job, overeating at home, and just not feeling up to doing anything at all (Lesson #3). That didn't stop the panther from wanting more, unfortunately, and the situation continued to deteriorate until I finally accepted that a mistake had been made and this panther had to go, like it or not (Lesson #4). The dismembering of the poor creature is not one of my happier memories, and I still sometimes miss my first-created, but I learned some lessons from that bit of foolishness about creating a familiar, the importance of focusing my thoughts sharply, being sensible about the image and size, some of the hazards of not being sensible, and, finally, how to destroy a familiar. You'll probably have to learn a lot of lessons the hard way, too, but don't let it deter you—we've all gone through something of the sort at one time or another.

This should serve well enough as an introduction to other beings. The elementals are pretty universal in their acceptance by different schools and traditions and can usually be counted on to be cooperative even if they're limited in abilities. Spirits and intelligences can be useful for simple work of any sort and their superiors—the angels and archangels—can be approached for more difficult or important work.

Animal familiars can be useful as well as being friendly, loving and cuddly. A real rapport can be established with animals if you give it a serious try and that in itself can prove very educational and satisfying.

If you can summon a spirit to serve as your familiar, keep it in a ring or some other article you can carry with you all the time so it's conveniently at hand whenever you need it. (Remember that physical room isn't a problem for a non-physical being.)

Finally, if you want to create your own familiar, be sensible enough to keep it small so you won't kill yourself trying to maintain it.

CHAPTER FIVE

Ethics and Morals

BEFORE WE GET INTO the matter of actually preparing and performing a ritual, it's time we give some serious consideration to the ethics and morals of magick and Wicca. People in the Craft, regardless of level, tradition or anything else, share a common belief in reincarnation. Just as other things in nature die and are reborn, so do people. Most believe it's the only rational explanation for so much that there's really no need to debate the question anymore. The growing popularity of the belief in reincarnation among those outside of the Craft is an encouraging sign that many—Christians, Moslems, and others—are discovering from within themselves that this is a valid belief and are trusting their intuitive feeling.

Reincarnation is intended to provide an answer to the question of what we're doing here. The great "Why?" That answer breaks down simply to a matter of finding our way back to where we came from—home, if you will. The idea is that all of us, like everything else in nature, originated as part of God/The One/ The Great Spirit/The Creative Force/The Great Unmanifest. Having originated in perfection we have to regain that perfection before we can return and reunite with it. It doesn't demand, as some religions do, that the state of perfection be achieved in one lifetime with eternal damnation in Hell being the price of failure (or ignorance). It took millennia to work our way down into the physical world to the extent we once were, and it will take millennia to work our way back again. All worthwhile things take time.

Some people believe that the concept of reincarnation goes against all church teaching. Strictly speaking, this isn't the case. Some evidence suggests that reincarnation was an integral part of early Christian belief that was later deleted from church teachings. By way of modern-day evidence I offer the following anecdote: Some years back, the Polish philosopher Professor Lutoslavski wrote a letter to the eminent Cardinal Mercier of Malines inquiring as to the position of the Catholic Church on the subject of reincarnation. The response, in part, was "The doctrine of reincarnation has never been formally condemned by the Roman Church as heretical." While reincarnation may not be openly promulgated by the church anymore, it is not incompatible with the beliefs of Catholicism.

The human race continues to evolve as a whole just as individuals evolve, and nature evolves on the physical plane. There's a spiritual evolution of the race as well as a physical evolution. Along the way we get a lot of help. Great teachers and masters such as Jesus and Buddha visit us from time to time, and individuals have spirit guides whom we often hear as our conscience.

Before I go any further on ethics and morals in magick, I'd like to present a disclaimer. There is no intent to teach a system of ethics. Most of what we learn as "proper behavior" is the working system of a particular society, with various peculiarities unique to that society. As a case in point, consider the Western position on suicide. For centuries it was considered an entirely appropriate response to various situations relating to honor. From the Roman Empire to Japan, it was not the act of a coward but rather the price of failure. It's all a matter of where and when you live.

As societies change, concepts of morality and ethics change, but they invariably involve the protection of the society as a whole, frequently at the cost of individual benefit. And while it can be argued that spiritual values are constant throughout time, it remains true that what is right and proper for individuals (and for the race as a whole) changes with spiritual evolution, so right behavior for me now might not be right behavior for you now, or for me a couple hundred years from now.

The following is intended to give you general information on what some believe, along with some things to keep in mind when asking yourself what you should or should not do. The answers aren't always easy to come by and sometimes they may not be the answers we may want. In the end, you've got to answer for yourself. If you take the time to quietly ask yourself whether or not something you want to do should be done, you'll get an answer. It's then up to you to (a) differentiate between what you want to do and what you should do, and (b) act accordingly.

The Threefold Law

Wicca has an official policy on morality, which is comprised of two elements: the "Threefold Law" and "Do what you will but harm none shall be the whole of the law. Love is the law, love under Will." The latter, as put by Aleister Crowley, is pretty clear. You can do anything you desire to yourself and you can do anything you want to with someone else as long as the other person is a willing participant, but don't do anything that in any way will harm a person who doesn't freely agree to it. That policy allows for a wide latitude while protecting everyone and everything.

The Threefold Law is: "Anything you do to another, whether it be for good or ill, shall be returned to you threefold." Some choose to add to that ". . . in this lifetime." Most witches don't curse everyone they don't care for because they believe the price is too high. If you curse someone it's going to come back to you, and then some. Let's say someone gets you angry and you decide to make the engine of his car blow up. You'd better be careful because your own car might get totaled (with you in it). Three times bad or three times good is what you can expect.

That's the official line in the Craft, although the Threefold Law on its face is a direct contradiction to the greater Law of Balance. One equals three does not compute. Also, karma is a law of cause-and-effect, the purpose of which is to teach, not punish. When trying to teach that an action or thought is "wrong," you don't use any more force than the minimum necessary to get the message across. (That's the Law of Conservation of Energy.) An unwavering policy of three-for-one, regardless of the act or need, is unnatural, unbalanced, and frequently overkill. It's the official policy, probably intended to keep neophytes in line.

Karma

The Law of Karma is a kind of guiding force behind the belief in reincarnation. Part of us knows what's right and wrong, regardless of what we're taught by parents, associates, laws or circumstances. When we die, we're judged by what we've learned (or forgotten) in the just-completed lifetime. I suspect we probably make that judgment for ourselves. Free of the effects of life in a physical body, we can step back and look at our personal history more objectively, with full memory of what we've done, what we intended to do, and what's still necessary for us to do to move along that path of reunification with Perfection. After a period of rest we decide what weaknesses we're going to confront next, then we come back into another body, and karma provides the opportunities for learning and growth.

Please note I said "learning and growth." I didn't say "punishment." Karma is meant to give us an opportunity to learn a lesson, not to pay a price, based on our past actions. Once the decision has been made as to what lessons are to be learned, karma will find a way of imparting those lessons. Regardless of how we change our lives, what we do with our lives, or what is done to us, karma will find a way of fulfilling its assigned task.

We choose to learn; karma provides us with the means to learn. It's not an intellectual knowledge, but something that goes deep into the soul to become an ingrained part of us. Some people, for instance, have to restrain themselves from hitting back at someone or from taking something they want that's within reach with no risk of being caught. Others never even consider the possibility. That's the difference between knowing something is wrong and *knowing* something is wrong. When we really *know* something, it becomes part of us, and the matter is closed. Karma is not a blind, driving force. When a lesson is truly learned, karma is satisfied. It doesn't matter if we've learned that lesson because of something which we've confronted *because* of karma or if we've learned it in some other fashion. A lesson learned is a lesson learned, and karma won't try to force a person to learn a lesson which has already been learned. If someone does something wrong, *feels* it's wrong, *knows* it's wrong, offers a soul-full atonement for it, and never has the slightest inclination to do it again, that lesson is learned. Case closed. Teaching, not punishment.

Responsibility

Tied in with karma is the question of sin. Sin is a religious word that relates to the question of right and wrong, as well as to karma. Sin can't exist without knowledge. Adam and Eve were free of sin until they obtained knowledge of what was right and what was wrong. It's not quite a matter of "ignorance is bliss," but it's a far cry from "ignorance of the law is no excuse." The more you know, the greater your responsibility for your actions.

Performing magick isn't a sin by definition. Hurting someone may be a sin, depending on knowledge and intent. If you proceed with something intending to hurt someone, or even knowing it might hurt someone, you're responsible. As you learn how to manipulate the forces around you, you're expected to know what you're dealing with and what laws apply. If you use magick for something negative, you'll pay a higher price than if you had done the same thing through non-magickal means. The higher the level at which you're working, the greater the penalties for being wrong. If you do anything that harms someone else, even if that isn't your intent, it will come back to you eventually.

Still, we're always faced with decisions, and sometimes we experience conflict between what we're expected to do and what we believe we should do. Moral conflicts aren't easy to face or resolve. The following story on this point comes from India:

Arjuna, while a human, ruled a land at war with another. On the eve of a major battle he was faced with choosing between his teaching that killing was wrong and the fact that the next day he was expected to send his army into combat where large numbers of people would be killed. He agonized over this conflict between his responsibility as warrior and his responsibility as a spiritual being until he finally received the guidance for which he prayed. As a being possessed of a physical body in this world he had certain responsibilities. These included leading, guiding, protecting and defending his people. To shun those responsibilities and refuse to do what had to be done for their sakes would be a greater sin than giving the command to enter the battle, in spite of all the deaths it would cause.

A more modern analogy would be the moral dilemma world leaders faced in choosing between sending thousands of people to death in a war or letting the Germans and Japanese march unopposed in World War II. Sometimes you will be faced with decisions you don't want to make, but as a human being you have a certain responsibility to your family, your friends and the rest of mankind. Sometimes that responsibility may put you in direct conflict with what you know is morally right. You are living in this world and you must function here and do what's best for everyone, or you will have failed to live up to the responsibility you've chosen to confront this time and will have to face it again at some point in the future. The concept of Honor relates to more than mere personal ego, pride or vanity.

You are responsible for the results of your actions, including an awful lot that you may not be aware of. Think about second-hand results. If you give someone a gun, show them how to use it, and they use it to kill someone, are you responsible? If you encourage someone to do something wrong that will get them into trouble instead of doing something to them directly, you'll still be responsible for that person's actions. You're responsible for your actions in all things according to both the laws of government and the law of karma.

Judging

We're here to learn our own lessons, not to judge the means by which lessons are imparted. A very important lesson for you to learn is don't judge. You have no way of knowing what other people need to learn, nor how they must go about learning it. Nor do you have any sure knowledge of whether or not you have a role to play in that lesson. Keep yourself apart. Don't judge. You may read in the paper about a murder and feel compassion for the victim (or the murderer, in some cases) but don't be too quick to judge right and wrong. It may have been the right time for the victim to die (meaning everything had been done that needed to be done in this lifetime); it may have been necessary for the victim to die by violence. That doesn't make it right, mind you. A premature, truly untimely death is a sad waste. It takes years and years to grow up again through infancy and childhood and to learn to function in a "new" society with a "new" language but it still isn't final. You can't know death wasn't the necessary act at the time.

You have to do what's right for *you*. Let's say you witness a crime. Commission of the crime actually may have provided some kind of lesson the criminal needed to learn. You don't know, so you can't judge him. It's possible that the crime was intended to fail, creating an opportunity for the criminal to learn something through the criminal justice system. You don't know that, either. You were told not to judge, so what do you do?

You do what *feels* right for you. If something inside you says you should intervene—maybe by stopping the criminal or providing an identification of him—that's what you do. Peer pressure and group pressure are all ultimately irrelevant. You have to look inside for the answer, knowing that you are responsible for your action or inaction, and not knowing if there's a lesson here, too. If you're a member of a law-and-order organization your response may seem clear; if you're a member of a street gang your response may be equally clear, though different. The expectations of others are not as important as what you need to do.

I'm definitely not encouraging you to take the easy way out, giving you a rationalization for not getting involved. It's too easy to let the person get away, arguing that someone else will stop him or, eventually, karma will get him if nothing else does. That's a cop-out. Others may think that getting involved is the only proper, civic thing to do. Go with your heart, not your brain. Do what you feel is right, not what you think or rationalize is right. I told you not to judge others, but you'd better judge yourself!

The question of right and wrong is not always simple and obvious. Sometimes we can look inside and not find the answer, so we have to resort to using our heads instead of our hearts. And sometimes our hearts are the source of the problem when we feel we need to do something but are not certain what is right. Right and wrong are not always black or white. Grey exists as the predominant color, and unless you're a Master, you're going to be confused sometimes and you're going to be wrong sometimes. But that's part of life.

The Dark Side

The term Satanism is mainly used for its shock value in our culture. Frequently it's used to describe individuals or groups that do not share the belief system of those applying the label. This is obviously nonsense, but often it can be (or is meant to be) dangerous nonsense. On the other hand, there are those who adopt the name for themselves precisely because of the shock value, with little or no knowledge of the workings of Satanism. In these cases it's an attention-getting device, sometimes productive, sometimes destructive, but either way usually successful.

Defining Satanism isn't as easy as many would have us believe. Certainly there are those who ostensibly worship an entity named "Satan" with the qualities and appearance ascribed by Christian traditions. In those cases, applying the term is easy, but they're few and far between, and generally these people know little or nothing about magick anyway. There are other cases where the entity being worshipped has a different name but the same qualities, which we can also consider a form of Satanism. In most cases, however, the issue is not the name of the central deity, or even the belief in a deity, but a philosophical attitude which many would call "satanic" and, therefore, call its adherents "Satanists." For our purposes, I'm going to use the lower case satanism to represent a general class of magickal practitioners who would be said to deal with the darker side of power. Keep in mind, however, that most people who call themselves Satanists have little, if any, true working knowledge of magick—they're just trying to shock you and/or get your attention.

This seems like a good point at which to address the issues of black magick and black magicians. One common phrase is that "there's no such thing as black magic, only black magicians." Another, which may be more appropriate, is that "nothing in the world is black or white, merely different shades of grey." As I've pointed out, questions of morals and ethics aren't always easy to answer. I personally don't know anyone who can say they've never done anything in their life which had a negative effect on someone else, so labelling someone "black" based on only what you perceive may be an unfair proposition.

There are two major differences between those who tend toward the dark side—satanists or others—and those who don't. First of all, these people often will frankly admit they're out to get all they can for themselves. Secondly, there's a difference in the primary source of energy these people draw upon for their work.

Philosophically, they aren't that much different from other people. Their basic premise is that they are going to take care of themselves first, family second, and friends third. They think they have a right to whatever they want, and if anyone or any-thing stands in their way it is going to get smashed. They're unconcerned about who may get hurt. Nature is based on survival of the fittest, they argue, and they are willing to do whatever is necessary to ensure that they survive and prosper. It's this willing-ness to advance self-interest regardless of the cost to others that defines the satanist. You probably know a few people who are satanists at heart, if not in practice, and one is no less dangerous to the world than the other.

The source of energy these satanists draw on, as I've said, is different than that used by other magicians: they draw power for their personal use from the life energies of people around them. Usually this is done in a controlled fashion to avoid arousing suspicion, but sometimes it's taken too far. Ethical and moral questions arise when the line is crossed and the psychic feeding becomes excessive. The victim is then left weak, debilitated, and, if the draining is not stopped, it can be lethal. (That's where we find the true roots of the vampire legends.) Sometimes this is done deliberately as a means of retribution; other times it's viewed as an unfortunate necessity, with the reasoning that "I" am more important than "you" and, therefore, if I need the energy and am capable of taking it, that's your problem.

To outsiders, these satanists are cruel, heartless, self-cen-tered, self-absorbed, evil and dangerous. To the satanist, outsiders are frequently evil, heartless, cruel, self-centered, self-absorbed, self-righteous, hypocritical, ignorant, and deserving of what they get. This is not said in their defense; I am trying to illustrate another point of view. What we're looking at here is a different set of moral and ethical standards. These people are a definite minority, but to them, their approach to life is the more natural one. As potential victims, you may feel differently.

Sacrifices

What about the use of blood sacrifices in magick? Don't Satanists do it? Isn't it a part of black magic? Forget it. It may be mentioned in a lot of books about magick, and certainly it's in a lot of movies, but that's just the movies. If you believe that a blood sacrifice is necessary to make your ritual work, you're barking up the wrong tree and obviously have a lot more to learn.

Voodoo, Macumba and Santería, among others, do use animal sacrifices. The practice of animal sacrifice can be traced from Abel to Abraham, right on through the entirety of the Old Testament, and includes virtually every tribe in the eastern Mediterranean on into India. Many Greek rituals involved the sacrifice of a goat, lamb or bull, and this practice was carried on in Rome well into the Christian era. What is often missed, however, is the fact that in every one of these religions and rituals, the sacrificer was held in a special relationship with his god. With the Jews, for instance, only the Levites were allowed to make sacrifices. Even today in the Afro-Catholic traditions mentioned above, the role of sacrificer is reserved for a specially trained elite, though still often with questionable results.

The use of blood sacrifices in both religious and magickal rituals fell into disrepute centuries ago. Obviously, if it was the easy, effective means to an end so many try to represent it as being, this wouldn't have been the case. Nothing significant happens without a reason, and there's a reason most magick doesn't include something as significant as blood sacrifice anymore: it proved generally ineffective and useless. The material included in this book presents not the remnants of old traditions, but the effective forms that have evolved from those traditions over the centuries. Blood sacrifices are not part of any of them and, as I said, if you think you need to kill something to get something, you've still got a lot to learn about magick and life.

It should be stated that valid arguments exist on behalf of all the forms of magickal and religious practice, though each of them has a prejudice against the others. One line of thinking is that the more you get away from pure mental work the lower and baser the form of magick, the implication being that the more you can do just through your mind the more evolved you are. It can also be argued that magick can and should involve the entirety of your being as a human, including the physical side, so the combining and integrating of the mind's abilities with a good, physical body and the directed use of sexual energies is the best way to go. Others say that the more dependent an individual is on mere sexual energy, the less evolved that person is. There is something to be said for this, since there's a tendency to divorce the rational mind from the magickal work in these traditions.

The use of a blood sacrifice was once a significant ingredient in all magickal works, and aside from the old books on magick you can verify it in the Bible. But we've come a long way since those days, and the human race has continued to evolve both mentally and spiritually. As I said, sacrifices were used for the energy they release, both in the victim and the executioner, and *at that time* the extra energy was important to making a ritual work. We don't need that now, even though it's still used in some places because of tradition and heritage, or because of convenience.

Let us take a higher road. The point of this book is the development and use of power, within the context of spiritual development. Don't lose sight of that, regardless of your intentions. You have a responsibility to *life*, not death; to promoting and protecting all life as part of nature, part of creation, and, hence, part of yourself. By deliberately making unnecessary death an integral part of your life you are working at cross-purposes with yourself and the cost may be very high. We've come far enough now as a race that you don't need sacrifices to be effective, so stay away from them.

The Tie That Binds

Any time you work magick or do something with or to another person, a tie is formed between you and that person or what you desire. Some of your energy goes out to that person and/or some of that person's energy comes to you to form the tie. The tie can be strong—a bond—or weak, but it's there.

When you really want something badly, your desire creates a tie to that thing, whether it's money, a car, or a person. The stronger the desire, the stronger the tie. This can work in your favor in terms of magick because you need that strong desire to make it work. On the other hand, if it doesn't work or the object of your desire is lost later on; the desire itself remains imprinted on another plane where it may continue to haunt you in future lifetimes. That desire becomes part of yourself, part of your karma, and stays with you until it is realized or released at some point in the future.

If your desire is for money, and if the desire is really strong but doesn't materialize in this lifetime, you'll continue to pursue it in another to the point that it may become a highly destructive obsession. If your desire for a particular person is not fulfilled in this lifetime, the tie you've created will cause you to encounter each other in another, when you and that person might come together. The trouble is the soul of that person may be the same, but the personality and physical being won't be. You might find yourself inextricably bound to someone you truly loathe. Keep that in mind before you put a lot of energy into getting someone you think you really want right now.

On the personal side, two people who begin working to-gether often end up married to each other or living together.

High Priests and High Priestesses are especially vulnerable to this and, in some traditions, are even required to marry. In working together a bond is formed through the exchange of energy that takes place and that bond stays with you indefinitely. I know many people who are together now in part because they were working partners in a past life.

People tend to forget that any exchange of energy creates a link. That applies to sex, too. In many parts of the world, while intercourse is not discouraged, there's a warning that accompanies oral sex. Male or female, the fluids that come from the genital organs are heavy with your energy and life force. If another person consumes any of it a link is created that can be used in the future to influence that person. In some cultures, for instance, it's believed that if a woman can get a man to drink any of her juices, she can use the resulting link to gain control over him for the rest of their lives. (For some reason they seem to ignore the fact that it works both ways.)

Of course, that's where the energy is most strongly concentrated during sex and it's the location of the source of life, which explains why it's thought to have a magickal influence. But the basic exchange of energies that accompanies most intercourse can also create a link, and the more often it happens the stronger the link becomes. Have you ever known a couple who seemed to hate one another but couldn't stay away from each other? How about people who are separated yet still seem to be obsessed with one another? Or how about the happily married couple who always seem to know what the other is thinking before a word is spoken? Part of it has to do with the link created through the sharing of their energies.

Before you go after a working partner, remember that something of that person is going to be a part of you for the rest of your life and part of you is going to be part of that person, too.

If you perform some act of magick directed at another individual, a link is created that you need to be prepared to either maintain, live with, or suppress to the point that it can be ignored. Also keep in mind that the other person can use that link as well as you can. That's a good reason for learning how to protect yourself from any kind of psychic or magickal attack: a link you've created can be used to trace back to you in kind.

The following is a hypothetical situation I've discussed with many people that has produced a lot of conflicting opinions, no two agreeing on all points:

A man, single, reasonably good-looking, intelligent, monetarily comfortable, with a good job, has some knowledge of magick and generally uses it constructively. He's really attracted to a woman but she ignores him because she's totally involved with another man who most others agree is not a good person. The man has a number of options: (1) he can bide his time, hoping they'll break up; (2) he can do a ritual to cause something to happen to the man; (3) he can do a ritual to cause one or the other to lose interest; (4) he can do a ritual to cause her to fall in love with him. Which way to go? Option 2 should be out because it violates the injunctions against harming someone and against making judgments of another person's actions. Let's say Option 1 is out because he doesn't have the patience or there's little hope that things will take the natural course he'd like. Option 3 is a legitimate choice, but still leaves a lot to chance. That leaves Option 4: the love ritual. (Yes, love rituals are possible, but I'm not going to present any in this book.)

Is it right or wrong for him to perform a ritual to cause her to fall in love with him if it is unlikely to happen without a ritual? It's extremely difficult, if not impossible, to interfere with another's karma. If the ritual succeeds, it can be argued that it was the proper thing for him to do. If the ritual doesn't work, it can be inferred that he wasn't intended to have her. Helping to remove her from a potentially dangerous relationship is another argument in his favor but passing that judgment on the relationship isn't, since you can't know if one is contributing to some lesson the other needs to learn or if they're working out a karmic tie. Openly interfering in the direction of her life also argues against his interference. Still, it's possible that the woman can provide him with something that he legitimately needs to progress, and that this relationship would not be destructive to her in any way, in which case it might be proper. It's also possible that he doesn't realize that it might have a negative effect on her, in which case he's asking for trouble based on our earlier discussion of responsibility. And there's the possibility that *his* karma can best be served by getting the woman, even if it means using a ritual to get her.

Finally, if it's good to feel love, and if being in love is a desirable condition, then isn't it good to make it possible for an individual to experience love regardless of what instills that emotion?

What's your verdict? Wait? Separate them and move in? Do the love ritual? I know full well that a lot of you may have checked out this book for love rituals first thing. The truth of the matter is that most people, when first investigating the possibility of learning magick, are looking for either curses or love rituals. I hope you've learned by now that it isn't that simple. There's a lot to take into consideration besides your immediate emotional or physical needs. Being alone might ultimately be a lot better for you in terms of your own development than having someone around that you got for the wrong reasons or with negative consequences for the other person, regardless of your intent. You don't just go around performing rituals for something you want without giving a great deal of thought beforehand to all the potential ramifications of your actions, looking at it from every possible point of view.

On the other hand, there's sometimes a tendency to get so caught up in debating a question that no action is ever taken. You've got to consider every option and the consequences of each possible action or inaction before committing yourself to a decision, but by all means make a decision, even if it's a decision not to act! Don't go on debating forever. Sometimes we have to act, even if there's a question of doing the wrong thing. We're living, dynamic human beings and we're learning something each step of the way. Making a wrong decision is better than making no decision at all, because we'll learn something from it. Putting your hand on a hot stove is a painful way to learn a lesson, but the lesson gets learned in the process.

While it's acceptable to pursue a path leading to power over all aspects of your environment, don't forget the equal reality of the other two paths—love and knowledge. You're not going to get very far by accenting one while deliberately ignoring the others. You can accent any one of them more than the others— that's to be expected—but the proper use of power should contribute to a greater understanding of yourself and the world in general, with an appropriate increase in the understanding of the paths of knowledge and love. Abusing one path for the sake of another will probably prove to be self-destructive in the long run.

Tolerance

I've said a great deal here concerning right and wrong from my perspective and from the Craft's perspective. Now I'd like to address the question of other religions. In most books on the subject which are written by pagans, there's a tendency to treat other religions, especially Christianity, rather harshly. This comes from the fact that paganism emphasizes personal freedom in behavior, free of guilt and sin, while the Church seems to have an historic tendency to consider pleasurable acts sinful. Another reason is that pagans were persecuted by the Church during, for instance, the witch trials of the Middle Ages and later. Pagans see the Church as historically hypocritical, lecturing on love and brotherhood and seeking the kingdom of God yet at the same time killing people around the world in pursuit of temporal power.

Love, knowledge and power are three paths to the same goal. Most religions are also trying to guide people to that same goal. Just as some people may need to follow the path of power rather than the path of love in this particular life, so others may need Catholicism or Islam rather than a nature-oriented religion like paganism. I don't know what each needs and I will not condemn anyone else for choosing the path they are on. You shouldn't, either. Each religion, paganism included, has committed wrongs at some point in its history, and the fault lies with individuals, not necessarily with the religion itself.

Just as many people are choosing to believe in reincarnation today in spite of what they were brought up to believe, each of us has to choose what we will or will not believe. Christians, regardless of sect, are not wrong in what they believe, nor are Jews or Moslems or Buddhists. In deciding when and where to reincarnate, probable religious upbringing is taken into account and either there's something about a particular religion that we need at the time or we abandon that religion for another when we are old enough and intuitive enough to realize we need something else. If any pagan traditions feel right to you, that's good. A lot of happiness and joy can be found there, and the respect and affinity for nature that comes with it is something we need a lot more of in the world. But always remember to leave others to their chosen paths. You can introduce them to yours, but if they don't agree, respect their choice.

CHAPTER SIX

Making It Work

ONE QUESTION TO ASK when trying to understand how magick works is "According to whom?" That's one very big question. Different people, different schools, different traditions—all have different thoughts and beliefs on this question. If someone succeeds in healing another, it's either magick, a miracle of God, an act of Jesus or of Satan, depending on whose opinion is being expressed. It's a matter of perspective, and perspectives can vary dramatically.

Before we get into this too deeply, I'd like to present a couple of the root concepts of magick—sympathetic magick and "As Above, So Below."

Sympathetic Magick

Sympathetic magick was probably the first type attempted. The idea behind it is that you can affect one thing/person by affecting something that is either similar to it or that contains something that was physically connected with it. Drawing a man spearing an animal is a form of sympathetic magick intended to make the hunt successful. Sticking pins in dolls fashioned to resemble a person is a form of sympathetic magick. Any time you read about getting a strand of hair, nail clipping, etc., sympathetic magick is afoot.

The latter example is based on the principle that everything in the world is connected with everything else in the world in some way. In magick, it's also believed that everything you come in contact with retains some of your personal energy, and things from your body have a great deal of this energy. Something done to your object/hair/clippings, traces back along the energy tie between it and you, causing the same thing to happen to you. Another aspect of this is reflected in clairvoyance. If you're psychic, or if you know anything about psychics, you realize it's frequently necessary to handle an object or piece of clothing belonging to a person in order to pick up information about that person. The personal energy built up in the object forms a psychic link that can be used to psychically tune in on the person.

As Above, So Below

The principle of As Above, So Below is said to have originated with Hermes Trismegistus (a Greek name meaning "the thrice greatest Hermes"), variously thought to have been a wise man, a magician of the highest order, a Master or the Egyptian god Thoth or Tehuti, the god of wisdom, learning and literature. It's possible that all of the above are true. Hermes also is called "the scribe of the gods" and the source of all sacred books, which is why many Western magickal traditions today are called "Hermetic," meaning the original source of information was Hermes.

As Above, So Below reflects the relationship between our physical world and the astral plane. In its simplest terms, it means that anything that happens on the astral plane has a corresponding effect on the physical plane. Our physical plane is one of form and emotions; immediately above us is the astral plane, a plane of force without form; above the astral plane is the mental plane, a plane of form involved with the mind. Above that is the spiritual plane, which is force, following the alternating pattern. All of these planes are interrelated so what happens on one has a direct influence on what happens on the others. For magickal purposes, As Above, So Below encourages the use of your mind and/or emotions to cause change on the astral plane. You create an image of what you want and use it to give a corresponding form to the forces of the astral plane; that form above then manifests on the physical plane below in an identical fashion.

Most people involved with magick would probably agree that all magick is mental in origin. Whether the mental energy utilized in the magickal act works directly on an individual or event, or first influences the astral plane is open to discussion and debate. I don't know, maybe both are right.

The questions of how and where magick works still need to be addressed. First, some magick is probably telepathic in nature. Using your mind you can certainly affect the way another person acts. Some old-time telepathy exercises include concentrating on someone to make them call you on the phone, or staring at the back of someone's head until the person turns around to look at you. These acts fit our technical definition of magick because they (1) cause a change in the environment (2) in accordance with will (3) through non-physical means. The principal variable is a matter of degree. Influencing someone to call you is one thing; getting someone to offer you a job is something else. The difference is only in the degree of influence you exert on the person in question. By developing your personal power and energy, focusing it and sending it out with the guidance of effective visualization, you can increase the degree of influence you exert on others.

Impinging and Molding Theories

In terms of affecting things through the astral plane—the As Above, So Below principle—there are different theories as to why it works and how to approach it. I'm going to label two of these as the Impinging Theory and the Molding Theory. What both of these have in common is the concept of a flow of energy around us and this flow having a general direction that can be changed. This notion is similar to the concept expressed by astrologers that "the stars impel, they do not compel," meaning that there is an innate direction events will take unless acted upon by outside forces. The corollary in physics is that an object in motion tends to travel in a straight line until acted upon by an outside force. Magick is intended to be that outside force.

The Impinging Theory holds that all you need to do is provide a little impetus to the energy flow to change its direction, causing it to go in the new direction you've chosen. The idea is that we're dealing with a flexible system and all it takes to change something is to impress our own ideas upon it rather than let it flow in its otherwise natural course. I call this "impinging" because it involves giving one push, then sitting back waiting for the results. The main element of this approach is that once you have placed the image of your Desired End Result into the system you basically should just step back, get out of the way and let the system work itself out. Don't worry about it, don't think about it, and don't repeat it because once is enough. Does it work? Is it enough? A lot of people are using it so it must be.

The Molding Theory perceives the system as more static and inflexible, yet malleable. While a natural flow of energy is believed to exist, that flow is somewhat harder to affect than the system described above. In this case you need to get into the system with all the energy at your disposal, tie in to the force and control it, molding it to your own specifications. While the Impinging Theory urges getting out of the way once you're done, the Molding Theory suggests constant involvement. All the energy you can put behind the image of your desired end result will go into the system to help form it into the image you've created in your mind. This is more in keeping with the As Above, So Below principle because you're trying to cause a deliberate change in the way things exist on the astral plane in the expectation that the change will reflect back to this plane.

Emotional forces can rise from the physical to the astral and mold the energies there into forms that then will reflect back. Mental forces can move down from the mental plane to the astral and, likewise, mold the forces into forms. These create the artificial elementals and thought forms. Since moving down from mental to astral can work, and going up from physical to astral can work, it stands to reason that a strong emotional force deliberately controlled and amplified by a strong will with sharp images can also work, and that's what the Molding Theory of magick advocates.

Should you address the problem once and let it go or keep pounding away at it until the system gives you what you want? If what you're working on is fairly simple and you can visualize it easily, in detail and with a lot of energy, once should be enough and I'd suggest letting it go from there. On the other hand, if you're working on something fairly major and you can recreate the image of it in your mind in exact detail on demand, I wouldn't hesitate to keep attacking it every chance I got on the theory that the more energy I put into something the more likely I am to get what I want out of it.

That's one approach to the theory of magick, looking at it primarily from a mental point of view. Most Wiccans and magicians would find either the Impinging or the Molding Theory, or both, acceptable. Another approach that deserves at least equal time involves the use of other entities.

Using Other Entities

Much magick—ceremonial magick in particular—utilizes other entities such as elementals, angels, demons, and deities of various orders to perform desired work. In these cases you're not working at influencing the system directly, but rather you're asking something else to affect it for you. The entity acts as an intermediary of sorts, taking your will and your general directions, then using its own resources to bring about the change you're specifying. You don't have to worry too much about how it's done, because you're leaving it up to the entity to decide on the most effective way of completing the task you've given it with the conditions you've set.

There's still the question as to whether the work is being done on this plane or the astral plane or even some other plane. For instance, is a familiar or an elemental, both of which have their existences on another level, causing a change to occur on their own plane or are they acting directly on the physical? Are they even capable of acting on the physical? Is an angel or demon working on its own level or on ours? I don't want to answer every question for you. Rest assured there is an answer, and you can get that answer for yourself. In fact, that will be one of your first exercises after you finish this book—determining which plane they work on.

I've made a number of references to storing energy. Storing energy is the placement of energy when it's available into a form from which it can be drawn later. Most of the deities mentioned can be used as sources of energy when doing magick. Through the ages people have put a lot of energy into those forms through worship rituals—much more than is needed to maintain them— and this excess energy can be drawn on in times of need. You can also create your own form, like a familiar, but one so basic and simple that little energy is needed to maintain it.

The application of this principle is quite simple. When you aren't doing anything in particular—on a break at work, at home watching television, or whatever—you visualize the form you're using as your storage battery and imagine all your energy going into that battery. Don't put so much in that you leave yourself feeling weak and tired, but invest any spare energy you have at the time, keeping in your mind the intent of storing it for later recall. In the future you'll be able to tap this as needed, whether to do magick (with or without a circle) or just to revitalize yourself when tired. You won't get it all back, mind you, because there will be some general dissipation, plus what's needed to maintain the image itself, but if you're using it regularly, there should always be enough stored for you to draw on when needed. Putting up your extra energy when you have it to spare costs you little and sometimes can provide that last added boost you need to make something succeed.

The Desired End Result

The first thing you have to do to work any kind of magick is to decide what you want to do. That can be a lot more complicated than you suspect. For one thing, you want to keep the necessary energy expenditure to a minimum: the less energy the work requires, the more likely it is to be successful and the less draining it will be on you personally. Another reason is covered by the admonition, "Be careful what you ask for—you may get it."

Keeping things simple requires careful definition and understanding of the desired end result, and most people really don't give it enough thought. Let's say you start with the idea that you want more money. Why? Let's say you want it to buy a house. Why? So you'll have a better place to live? So you'll save on rent? So you can get away from the neighbors? So you can have more room? See? It's not really the money you want, or even the house, but rather something the house will provide you with that you don't have now.

Then you have to carry the questioning even further. What constitutes a better place to live? What would it have that you don't have now? Or what would you gain by saving on rent? Why do you want to get away from the neighbors? Why do you want more room? Again, it's not really the house that you want but something the house will provide you with that you don't have now.

You can carry this exercise even further. If the new house had something that made it a better place to live, what would that mean to you? How would you feel if you got away from the neighbors? What would having more room mean for you? The bottom line will always end up being a feeling or emotion. What you want is to be more peaceful, to be more comfortable, to be more secure: ultimately, to be happier.

Consider the same chain of thinking as it might pertain to a man who thinks he wants a new sports car. Why? Maybe because of the image it will give him. Why? Because it may attract more women. Why? Because he desires more women, or a particular woman, around him. Why? Because they make him feel happy or good. So does he want the car or does he want pleasurable companionship? Using the same example but a different chain of logic, he wants the car because of the feel of power and freedom he can experience with a high performance sports car. Why? Because he doesn't feel as strong, free and in control as he'd like to. Why? Because something in his life is controlling him instead of the other way around. So does he want the car, or does he want to get rid of a boss, a dead-end job or a wife?

It's important to know exactly what it is you want because if you don't there's no way you're going to be able to communicate your true desire to anyone or anything else. Another reason is that everything ultimately comes down to a feeling, and that feeling should be an intimate part of all the visualizations and meditations involved with your magickal work because it helps to define the desired end result.

The addition of an emotional element to the desired end result has a direct bearing on the warning "Be careful what you ask for—you may get it." Using the earlier example, let's say you kept everything very general and simply concentrated on getting more money. Consider all the ways you could possibly obtain the money you're asking for: your house burns down, you lose everything you've accumulated all your life—souvenirs, mementos, photographs, the whole bit—but you do collect on the insurance. Your spouse/parent/best friend dies suddenly and unexpectedly of a mysterious illness and you're a beneficiary in the will. You're in an automobile accident that breaks both arms, both legs and your spine, leaving you paralyzed from the neck down but with a $5,000,000 insurance settlement. Well, you would have gotten the money you wanted.

See why being specific is important? Adding the emotional element to the visualization of the desired end result can help: a feeling of peace and happiness doesn't go with a state of mourning. Adding that positive emotional element can help (not guarantee, just help) to prevent anything negative from happening in connection with what you really want.

So far you've been presented with a lot of warnings, injunctions, and other statements intended to discourage you from certain negative acts. Now I get to give you some real encouragement.

In the movie *Wall Street*, the most often quoted scene has Michael Douglas proclaiming his creed that "greed is good." Well, he was close. Actually, "ambition is good." Self-advancement is good. Helping yourself is good. Guilt is not good.

Many people seem to believe that using anything of a magickal or psychic nature for their own personal benefit is a no-no and that the result would be either ineffectual or self-destructive. This may have something to do with the Christian doctrine of self-sacrifice and self-denial, but it's just not so. You can use magick to help yourself, socially, financially, and medically. Working for your own benefit is perfectly all right.

Think of it this way: there's plenty of everything for everyone in the world, it's only a question of distribution. Whether you're talking about food, money, housing or energy, you are entitled by fact of birth to a certain share of it, though prior life indiscretions may limit the size of that share. The use of magick to affect the system of distribution is acceptable as long as you don't overdo it. Consider letting the system work things out in its own way. Use it to attract your fair share, then let it be. Work for what you legitimately need and don't get carried away. Self-improvement is good; greed is not good.

For any of a number of reasons, you may not get everything you ask for, but if something doesn't work the first time, keep on trying. Maybe a change in the quantity or timing of the request, or maybe the ritual itself, needs to be altered. Then if something still isn't working for you, find out why it's not working. You'll find out later some ways of doing that, and I'd suggest you use them because you never want to accept failure as a matter of course: if something doesn't work, find out why.

The Witches' Pyramid

What does it take to make a magick ritual successful? The best place to start is with a concept referred to as "The Witches' Pyramid." The pyramid form is one of the strongest, most durable shapes known, which probably has something to do with why it was chosen for this symbolic lesson. The pyramid has four sides, and in magick these are labelled as "Will," "Imagination," "Faith" and "Secrecy." These are the four elements that go into all successful magickal workings.

Will is something we've been discussing. It's not enough simply to know what you want, you've really got to want it. You should want it so badly that you can sit down and fill your mind with nothing but that one thing, almost to the point of obsession. You have to be able to define your desire precisely and be able to concentrate all of your energy on the idea of obtaining that end. If the desire isn't strong then the motivation and force largely will be lacking.

A deep-seated desire is one of the strongest motivating forces for concentrating the will, which makes it the best starting point for a beginner. Certainly will encompasses a great deal more than just desire. Concentration comes into it, along with visualization. Concentration is what takes that desire and forms it into something that can utilize the energy you put into your magickal effort. Will provides the impetus, allowing all the power you can generate to bring life to your visualization and to send the image plus the energy out into the system so it can materialize.

Visualization provides the image. Energy provides the means. Will throws the switch to set everything into motion.

Imagination

The second side of the pyramid is imagination. In the course of preparing to do a ritual, and while actually performing it, you will spend a lot of time on visualization, which is where imagination comes into play. I'm talking about creating a sharp image in your mind of exactly what it is you want to accomplish each step of the way, from creating the circle you'll be working in, to doing the work itself, to storing the circle when you're done. Before you even cast the circle you will be preparing yourself mentally and physically, including taking time to picture in your mind just what it is you're trying to do.

You need to see your desired end result in exact detail, sharp and clear. If it's a house, then see yourself in that house. See the rooms, the furniture, the decorations, the appliances, the landscaping, the driveway and everything else that should be in, on and around the house, including yourself. If it's a car, see the color, the upholstery, the wheelcovers, the dashboard, the time on the clock. Feel the steering wheel and the vibration as you drive it. Get every detail of the picture, even down to how it makes you feel.

Once you have this image sharply in mind, you need to put every bit of energy you can into it and send that image out into the universe. You are trying to change the flow of the system—the astral plane—in such a way that it puts you where you want to be. (If you're trying to influence someone or something not including yourself, it still works the same way.) Whether you're working by yourself, trying purely mental magick, or working in a circle alone or with someone else, or whether your circle utilizes a Wiccan format or a ceremonial one, the principle of projecting a specific image of the desired end result remains the same.

This process has something of karate in that you want to put as much force behind your effort as you can, but you also need to concentrate that force. In karate, a small amount of force applied properly to the right spot can be much more effective than twice as much force applied to the wrong spot. The same is true with

magick. The amount of force you use is important, but the direction of the application of that force through your visualization
and applied will is what makes the difference between success
and failure.

Another good analogy is the story of the piece of straw found
imbedded in a tree after a tornado. The force of the wind applied
just right to the straw made it possible for that flimsy piece to
penetrate bark and wood. If the force of the tornado had been
applied differently, to the side of the straw rather than the end,
you'd merely have a flat piece of straw that hit a tree and fell to
the ground. The same amount of force would have been applied,
yielding different results.

When visualizing the image of what you want, the timing
you put into it is very important. Notice I said "timing" and not
"time." This means that everything must be in the present tense.
If you think in terms of "I want," then you'll continue to want.
If you think in terms of "I'm going to get," then at each moment
you're "going to get" what you want and never actually get it.
Avoid thinking in the future tense, with something in the process
of coming to you, or it will always be in the process of coming to
you. If you put it into the system as something that will occur in
the future, then it will always remain in the future and will never
come to pass.

You may have trouble visualizing what you want, particularly
when you're just beginning and you don't have much experience
or practice at it. If that happens, don't worry about it, just keep
working at it. On the other hand, once you can visualize what
you want with sufficient sharpness, clarity and detail, and you
find that there's one particular end result you have an inordinate
amount of trouble visualizing, it may be meant as a warning that
you should drop it. Entities of many levels and degrees keep track
of us, individually and as a race. Some things just aren't meant
to be for some reason unknown to us and if you try to make them
happen you'll find yourself thwarted at every turn.

Be sure that you really want what you think you want. Not
only do you run the risk of getting it on terms other than what

you'd like, but also it takes a lot more energy to undo something than it took to do it in the first place. You not only have to change the system back to what it was, but also have to override the energy that you put into changing it in the first place. If you put everything you had into the initial change, then you're going to have serious problems undoing it.

Finally, be careful about fantasizing. Whether you tend towards daydreaming or explicit sexual fantasies accompanied by masturbation, you're visualizing a situation different from your existing one, focusing and concentrating your attention on it, then putting an emotional force behind it all. While the conscious intent to create change on the astral plane is lacking, all other ingredients for magick are present and the emotional energy and/or repetition put into the visualized fantasy could be more than enough to bring it to actuality in spite of intent. Remember that the forms you're creating on the astral plane can directly affect this world; you could even become the victim of possession by one of your own creations.

Faith

Faith is an element we often mistakenly take for granted in discussions of magick. Faith exists on the emotional, rather than intellectual, level. It's really easy to say you've got to have faith in what you're doing, but it's not that easy to keep the faith. If your first five rituals are all productive, you will easily develop faith in what you've learned and your ability to use it. If none of them work, you'll probably decide magick is all nonsense and give up. Faith is either learned in youth or gained through personal experience. Nothing in any other book can provide you with faith in the validity of magick or anything else. Once you *experience* a successful magickal operation you'll begin to lay the groundwork for true faith.

If faith is one of the four sides to the pyramid required to be successful, and it doesn't exist until after a success, what can you do? Let's just say that disbelief will be counterproductive, guaranteeing failure. At the beginning you need an open, objective attitude geared for testing and experimentation without prejudging the results. Not everything you try will work, especially when you're just starting out. By experimenting with different methods in different situations you should eventually find a working system that will be productive for you, but it may take some time, effort and a lot of practice.

Magick is a science, much like physics. It consists of various laws and principles relating to the effects of energy on elements of the physical world and uses observation, trial and error, and repeatable experiments to deduce and test its theories and practices. The only real differences are that magick doesn't use any tools other than the mind, and its effects are not subject to measurement by any kind of instruments. If you approach magick through the same scientific method used for physics, testing the assumptions and observing the results, faith isn't really necessary. Faith will come in time, boosted by positive results. As long as you accept the possibility and work at determining what you personally need to do to make it effective for yourself, faith can be put aside in favor of dispassionate objectivity.

Secrecy

The last side of the pyramid is secrecy. The importance of maintaining secrecy relates to two principles we've already discussed: the ability of energy to affect the system and the element of faith. Say you attempt some magick, then tell someone else about it. They'll probably think you're crazy and that there's no way it can work. That reaction will send a lot of negative energy into the system that you've just been trying to affect. They'll really believe that it's not going to work, they'll have faith it's not going to work, and they'll express that faith with a lot of energy, and they'll see things remaining just as they are. Unconsciously, they'll be putting everything that is required to perform magick into the idea that your magick isn't going to work. The outcome will depend on whose magick is stronger.

If you're new to this and depending on keeping an open mind rather than relying on established faith, you may start questioning the effectiveness of your magick yourself. If everyone around you is saying you aren't capable of doing something, you'll take it to heart to the extent that, even if you do attempt to work magick, you won't put everything you've got into it and you will fail. So the element of secrecy is intended to protect you from yourself as well as from others.

On the subject of secrecy, it's time to get back to the subject of sympathetic magick. Sympathetic magick is where you work with something similar to or directly related to the person or thing at which the magick is directed. Voodoo has a strong element of sympathetic magick to it. If you're doing magick directed at a person, does that person have to know about it? Does it contradict the principle of secrecy if you tell that person about it? It depends on the person and what you're trying to do.

If a love ritual is directed at a strong-willed person who's deeply involved with someone else, I'd say don't tell that person about your ritual. At best it'll be laughed off, and at worst you'll create a level of resentment and animosity that no ritual can overcome. The key element here is the person's suggestibility, which is what Voodoo's success is partly attributed to. People in our society have less of a belief in magick, Voodoo and Macumba than do the Caribbean or Latin American peoples. If the person you're addressing doesn't believe you have any knowledge of magick even in theory, let alone in practice, then you've got a chance. A few well-chosen words and references should be enough to indicate that you know something about the subject.

Most people want to believe in magick and miracles. They want to believe that anything is possible in this world, and this desire to believe can be a kind of trump card for you. Suggestibility. Keep up the other three elements of the pyramid in everything you do with that person. If you act like you are willing it to work, and you communicate how you imagine it's going to be and show you have faith it's going to work, you can play on the person's suggestibility to the extent that you may arouse their interest. After all, people want to be wanted and desired, and if you show that much interest and determination, they will give you some kind of encouraging reaction.

Still, you have to know your target well. Generating open hostility won't help your cause one bit. Telling someone you've been sticking pins into a doll you've made of them won't do anything more than get you the blame for anything that does happen to occur. As a general rule, maintaining secrecy about your rituals is the safest and most productive way to handle them until the results are in. My comments in the first chapter urging people to come out of the closet referred to work already done or work to be attempted to help someone. The need to keep your activity secret is intended to avoid any interference while your desired end result is working itself out.

The Use of Ritual

Once you know what you want to accomplish and the basic elements of what's going to make it come true for you, you have to decide how you're going to utilize everything you've learned so far. That brings us to the matter of the use of ritual for performing magick. If everything is in the mind to begin with, why would we go through all the time, effort and expense needed for a proper ritual?

Ritual serves a number of useful purposes, regardless of whether a pagan or ceremonial approach is used. Each ritual puts you on a path blazed by others before you. Certain processes are known to make magick easier and safer, such as the Lesser Banishing Ritual, the consecration of the elements, the casting of the circle, etc. If you decide to use one of the pagan traditions, the trappings and the ritual help put you into contact with the deities of that tradition, who will lend their energies to your work. If you decide to use the ceremonial approach, you have to use ritual because it's the only path that's been paved to the entities involved. While it may be possible to summon them through mental means without any ritual, historical precedent has determined that they'll respond more readily to the proper formalities.

However, anything is possible. There is no irrevocable, immutable law that says the entities associated with ceremonial magick will respond only to a ceremonial ritual. Some, if not all, will respond almost automatically once you're in the proper frame of mind, with the conscious intention to call them. You may be able to get them to cooperate with your desires without going through a formal ritual, but the strength of your will and the nature of your desired end result will have a bearing on your success. I wouldn't say you absolutely can't summon and successfully direct such an entity without going through the full ritual process, but it's unlikely.

Ritual is intended to help put you on the path of least resistance and make your work easier. Another reason for using a ritual is purely a personal, psychological one. Ritual is intended to help you gain access to that part of your mind that can make contact with something inside and outside yourself. It opens the mental pathway to some of the other planes of life and knowledge with which we don't normally have any conscious contact. Most of us have some experience with religious ritual, so by utilizing a form of ritual for magickal purposes we're tapping into that experience to help us obtain the proper frame of mind, taking advantage of our own pre-existing mental conditioning. Likewise, the more often you perform a ritual, the more conditioned your mind becomes to entering the appropriate state for concentrating on your desires, making it easier to visualize your desired end result, and for contacting other entities.

People have always needed ritual to function. Various churches have established rituals that put us in a more religious frame of mind. But we've also got personal rituals. Every morning you get up, wash, dress, maybe fix some breakfast, and then go to work. Some days you wake up so tired you can't even think straight, but still you get up, wash, dress, maybe fix some breakfast, and then go to work. It's a morning ritual you follow automatically, even if you're not awake enough to think about it. The routine—the conditioned behavior—gets you through.

Mental attitude is everything in practicing magick. If your mind isn't into it properly, if your will isn't focused, if you're distracted so your imagination can't produce the detailed visualization necessary, you don't stand a chance. Ritual helps you to do all that. Ultimately, much ritual practice can be explained in terms of autohypnosis.

I've referred a number of times to the proper state of mind. Remember the story in the first chapter about a magician who's conditioned to trigger that portion of his mind associated with performing magick just by putting on his robe? That's what ritual will do for you. I can't really explain what the proper state of mind is or what it feels like. It includes relaxation, concentration, a feeling of deliberateness and determination, an element of quiet expectation, and a kind of expansion that makes you feel like your mind and senses extend well beyond your physical body. Some say it involves lowering your brain wave frequency into the alpha range or lower.

All magick involves going into yourself, whether you're attempting mental magick or ritual magick. You may think in terms of reaching out to things you can't see, or manipulating energies around you, but you're still going into yourself to find that part of yourself capable of reaching out. Your everyday, conscious mind is not what's involved in performing magick. This is the heart of magick, rather than the mind of magick. If you're calling on a deity or an angel or an elemental, it's not just your voice that's making contact, it's your mind, heart and spirit. If it was just your voice and a few words you wouldn't need any book on magick, and magick wouldn't be an occult art, but rather another aspect of day-to-day living.

Another psychological aspect of ritual to keep in your mind is that the ritual itself acts as a center of attention for everyone involved. All those in the circle are focusing on the same thing at the same time as the ritual is proceeding. This helps to create something called a group mind on the astral plane, imbued with all the emotions and intentions of those in the group. In a way it's rather similar in creation-style and makeup to a familiar.

This group mind can affect the emotions of the group, strengthening them and making it easier to concentrate and get into the work being done. This greater concentration puts more energy into the group mind. The process goes back and forth until the group disbands at the end of the ritual. The group mind is similar to the mob mentality or crowd mentality that occurs when a group of people in the same place, at the same time, focus their attentions on the same object, and end up thinking and acting in ways they'd never consider if left as isolated individuals. A group mind can be a powerful influence on the members of the group that created it.

A group mind can be a valuable tool if you know how to create and handle it consciously. The concept of the group mind is important to remember in day-to-day affairs as well, because it can come into being any time a group of people is focusing on the same thing, such as at a sporting event or a concert. While the creation of a group mind is easy and natural, requiring no real conscious effort, using it and controlling it to aid you in your work isn't so easy. As time goes on other sources can help you learn more of what to do with a group mind.

Ritual is an aid to magick. For the newcomer, it's a vital, indispensable aid. Later, as you gain more success in using a ritual method for performing magick, you may use less of it. Eventually you may be able to dispense with it completely. For some of you, the basic principles of what magick is and how it works will be all you need to work effectively and most of what comes between here and the last chapter of this book will be totally unnecessary. I've got one old friend who is a witch but who doesn't use any formal ritual at all and never has. Maybe you're like her. If not, I suggest you take advantage of the paths available through the use of different ritual techniques to make things easier on yourself.

Which Way to Go

The first choice you've got to make is how you're going to work. Are you going to a pagan/wiccan tradition, ceremonial, both or neither?

The pagan approach has the benefit of well-trodden paths behind it. Whether you prefer Celtic, Egyptian, Babylonian, American Indian, or whatever, those who have gone before you have put their energies into the images from which you'll be drawing. Whichever goddess or god you choose to work with, the energies of thousands of other people have been stored there and have been drawn upon for centuries before you, easing the path. You may gain a certain internal satisfaction and a new respect for nature and life from the pagan approach. You may start taking new pleasure in walking in fields and forests or looking at the crescent moon. On the other hand, maybe none of that will ever mean anything to you, in which case, I suggest you forget it.

Ceremonial magick might suit you better. For those who care to hold to Judeo-Christian traditions, this will do nicely. You may find a certain comfort or sense of power in dealing with familiar figures and images like Michael, Gabriel, Raphael, etc. Use of the traditional names of God might be more comfortable on your lips than Isis or Diana or Cerridwin. You may have more confidence in asking for help from archangels you're already familiar with than from a goddess or god that's new to you. That's okay. Many people find that they feel more in control with the summoning and commanding of spirits, and the sense of power that comes with that would certainly contribute to any kind of work you may intend to do.

You always have the option of not using any of the above. You have plenty of energy and power in your own body and mind without necessarily resorting to the use of other entities. The development of your internal abilities and the use of your mind could be quite enough. The bottom line remains "It's all in your own mind." Some consider the use of ritual—pagan or ceremonial—to be nothing more than a crutch that can and should be dispensed with; others find ritual useful. You make your own decision.

Let's say you want to try a pagan tradition. You've got the whole world from which to choose a model! Most cultures have had a pantheon of deities and magickal practices in their past, and most come from Europe, the Middle East, Egypt, North and South America. Because of racial, cultural and historical differences, few of the general public end up trying to learn the magickal systems of the American Indian or the various systems, such as Voodoo and Macumba, developed by their southern neighbors. The system of sorcery and personal power used by don Juan is attractive to many people, considering the number of books written and sold by Castaneda, but it's difficult to learn without one-on-one instruction such as Castaneda himself had.

Also, some traditions are highly specialized, emphasizing different aspects of paganism or having particular, selective memberships. Some, for instance, acknowledge no specific deity, but rather consider nature as a whole to be divine. One branch, referred to as the Dianic, is strongly feminist in nature and generally open only to women; still others are limited to gays, male and/or female.

If you choose one of the pagan traditions, learn the symbolism associated with that system and surround yourself with the appropriate trappings if you (safely) can. You can obtain artwork depicting the deities of various religions. Thanks to the renewed interest in Egypt resulting from the touring of the King Tut and Rameses III exhibits, you can buy and display a lot of drawings, statuary and such without causing embarrassing questions. For most of the others you'll probably need to contact a store that deals in Craft supplies.

Read some books specific to the tradition you want to try. Learn the mythology, the different deities, their names, attributes and relationships to each other. In this context, though, a word of caution: the Celtic tradition is very varied, has no written history, and has so many branches and branches of branches that you may run into some trouble, yet more books have been written based on Celtic traditions than any other.

You'll recall the earlier reference to Gerald Gardner in Britain, and some of the traditions that sprang from it such as the Alexandrian and Seax Wicca. There are others, of course, and they have certain elements in common, yet they have political differences, religious differences, differences in opinion, and none of them have verifiable historical roots. Presumably each has a system that has proven effective magickally based on experimentation and experience. The fact that Alex Sanders, for instance, doesn't have a written history as old as Egyptian or Greek civilization doesn't mean his system doesn't work.

Many Celtic traditions are actually Greek-based. You'll find the image of Diana popping up all over the place. This may, in part, be attributed to the extent of our knowledge of Greek mythology. It may also reflect the assimilation of Greek mythology by the Romans, and the subsequent spreading of that religion by the Roman armies. Also, there is a grace and beauty associated with the Greeks that seems more attractive than the deities of the true Celts. While there are certainly many corresponding images, Greek mythology elicits images of flowing white robes and marble columns while the Celts are pictured more in forest groves.

As you get more into the subject of magick and find more books available, you will run into a lot of grimoires and Books of Shadows. A few words of warning may be appropriate. Keep in mind that only scholars, most notably college professors, have to write books. Everything else, fiction and nonfiction, is a commercial effort. People who write books do so with a personal goal. Take everything with a grain of salt. Don't accept anything at face value. Keep an open mind, but always question the author's motivation for writing the book in the first place. Don't assume that anyone is always right, or even ever right, regardless of their degree of authority; that there's only one path that will work; or that one way is better than another for everyone. Don't take anything for granted as gospel truth, including this book. Look inward to your own intuition.

Books you read will tend to elicit one of three immediate responses in your head and heart: "that sounds right to me," "that sounds like bullshit," or "I don't know about that." At every step of the way, you have to depend primarily on your own intuition to guide you. Use that same intuition when judging anything you read, regardless of the source. Experiment to find what works best for you. Trust to your intuition. You may read something that sounds accurate but not *right*, which probably means the information is good but it's not for you. Just as many people today are picking and choosing from different aspects of various religions to put together a personal philosophy that feels right for them, treat everything you read about paganism and magick the same way: pick and choose what feels right for you, then use it.

One last point on Wicca before we get into the question of ceremonial. Your choice is not irrevocable, nor is it even limiting. You can try a number of different traditions before you settle down to one in particular, but that doesn't mean that once the choice is made you're committed to using only that tradition. Specialize in one, but keep an open mind, and don't be afraid to experiment.

Think of a tradition as being like a country. Each is separate, has its own rulers and subjects, has its own strengths and weaknesses, and each ruler has power only in his own country (though he may not be totally without influence elsewhere). If someone in country A does something the ruler of country B doesn't like, there's not much he can do about it. The time could come when you want to perform some particular work of magick, but based on your general knowledge, you know that tradition B has a deity better suited to the task than your own tradition A. What do you do? Move! If country B offered you better on-the-job working conditions than A you'd consider moving, wouldn't you? You may be more familiar with A than B, but if you understand the principles involved, with a little effort you can work in any tradition.

The other reason for remaining flexible is a defensive matter. Some people involved with magick are concerned only with now and don't consider or care about long-range ramifications of their actions. They do what they please to whomever they please. Or, at least, they try to. If you happen to cross one of them, you could be in for some trouble.

Generally, the principle suggested in my analogy about the powers of rulers of countries applies here: power directed through one tradition usually will be ineffective against the power of a different tradition. If you can find out what system of magick is being used against you, then defend yourself using that same system, your chances of success will be greatly enhanced. That should be an added incentive for you to study traditions other than the one you finally select for yourself and get some experience with their deities and symbols.

Regardless of the magickal system you use, try to limit yourself to a defensive posture rather than getting involved in a counter-attack. As with any dispute, escalation is a sure way of guaranteeing that everyone gets hurt. One of the most common methods of defense is to surround yourself with a shield of energy charged with the idea of reflecting anything trying to penetrate it. Create the shield with your mind, and as you're doing so, will it to send back to any attacker that which is being directed at you. This mirror defense can be quite effective. Finally, one of the best books I've found addressing the particular subject is *Psychic Self-Defense* by Dion Fortune.[6]

On the ceremonial side there's less flexibility in choice. Most schools associated with ceremonial magick trace their roots back to the Qabalah (also spelled Kabbalah and many other ways), although some credit Egyptian mystery schools, claiming these were distinct from Qabalistic tradition and merely share some similarities. Probably the most famous, or infamous, ceremonial

---

[6]Dion Fortune, *Psychic Self-Defense* (York Beach, ME: Samuel Weiser, 1977).

group was called the Golden Dawn. Most of what you'll find written in the 20th century has roots in that group. Israel Regardie has written a number of books about The Golden Dawn, its history and teachings.[7] The Rosicrucians claim descent from the Egyptian schools, as do the Masons. Since both organizations are still functioning with large, easily contacted memberships, you can investigate their claims and suitability for yourself with little difficulty.

The most well-known name to come out of the Golden Dawn was Aleister Crowley (who liked to say his name rhymed with holy); one of his most notorious books is *Diary of a Drug Fiend.*[8] Crowley experimented with just about everything in trying to master the magickal arts, including heavy use of drugs and sex. By popular standards he'd be considered a totally immoral man; he was something of an egomaniac and often relished offending people. On the other hand, many considered him to be an accomplished magician. Much of what he wrote deserves serious consideration by anyone inclined to ceremonial magick. The group he founded, generally referred to as the O.T.O., still exists, though there's been a schism with each group claiming to be the legitimate heir.

As with pagan writings, everything having to do with ceremonial magick is open to interpretation and questioning. Plenty of books on the subject provide instructions, guidance, rituals and the like, and some go so far as to provide drawings of demons. Most of these books have been subjected to copying, recopying, translation, interpretation, modification, and editing. Like the Bible, it's impossible to say how much is fairly attributed to the accredited author, how much is valid, and how much has been added or deleted by others for their own reasons. In any event, the best thing to do is read as much as you can, take all of it with

---

[7]See, for instance, Israel Regardie, *The Golden Dawn* (St. Paul, MN: Llewellyn Publications, 1971).
[8]Aleister Crowley, *Diary of a Drug Fiend* (York Beach, ME: Samuel Weiser, 1970).

a grain of salt, then experiment to see what will and will not work for you.

Ultimately, you should try to pick one particular way of working and stick to it, but you don't have to feel pressured to commit yourself too early. You may think based on what you've read, that Celtic paganism doesn't do anything for you, yet you might feel differently if you actually tried it. The same holds true for ceremonial. You have a lot of history rolling around in that subconscious mind of yours that you're probably completely unaware of, but which could end up having a dramatic effect on your work once you connect with it. Give everything a chance at least once. In the end, you'll decide what feels right for you. No matter which way you decide to go, keep working on the mental side of magick using meditation and visualization even in your day-to-day life. Practice helps, and nothing you do in the way of mental exercise is ever wasted.

If you happen to decide on a pagan tradition for your work, a large number of books is available to provide more specific detail on a range of them. A good general book is *Drawing Down the Moon* by Margot Adler.[9] It covers a lot of territory and has been updated with a listing of groups around the country. Also, if you contact one of the major occult suppliers, such as Llewellyn Publications in St. Paul, Minnesota, or Samuel Weiser or The Magickal Childe in New York, they can supply you with books and supplies, and fill you in on publications printed by individual groups around the country.

Solo, a Partner or a Group?

Once you've decided which approach you're going to try, you need to decide whether you want to work with anyone else. Probably as many people work solo as work in groups, and just about everyone who works in a group also works solo.

[9]Margot Adler, *Drawing Down the Moon* (Boston: Beacon Press, 1987).

You may not know anyone else who's interested in learning about magick, or you may not want anyone to know of your own interest. If that's the case, you'll have to go it alone. If someone close to you is willing to give it a try, so much the better. Or you could try connecting with an existing group.

In large part it depends on you. Some people just don't feel comfortable working with a group. You may not like having other people around you because they make you feel uncomfortable. If that's the case, by all means work solo. After all, if you're working with others and you don't feel comfortable with them, not only will you fail to bring yourself up to maximum effective power, but also you'll be a weak link for the others and may interfere with their efforts. If having other people around distracts you too much from concentrating on your work, you'd be better off working alone.

Working with a Group

Working with a group has advantages and disadvantages. Ideally, all members of the group would become close friends, feeling completely at ease with all the others. In a good group a rapport exists so everyone is open to the others; this permits the energy to flow freely and unencumbered. All else being equal (which it rarely is), the amount of energy generated by a group increases geometrically in proportion to the number of people in the group. (Two people working together will produce more energy than the combined energies of each working alone; five people working together will produce more than five times the energy of any one of them, and so on.) Also, you may feel more comfortable as part of a group working with others, so you'll be able to concentrate better and will generate more energy yourself.

Other good reasons for being involved with a group go beyond the question of working together. Aside from gathering for teaching, learning and practicing magick, groups usually also serve as social outlets for their members. Expect some changes in your personality and relationships as you become more involved with magick. You will find that people who don't share your interest more and more are kept at a distance and those relationships slowly die. It's as though there's an innate awareness that people who can't or won't understand your beliefs and attitudes aren't going to understand anything else of importance about you, either. If you can't discuss your interest in magick or psychism, the rest really doesn't matter enough.

That means old relationships are probably going to fade away and new ones will develop. But developing new ones based on your new interests can be difficult, especially if you remain hesitant to let on to anyone about your interest. Being part of a group for many people becomes their primary social outlet, and the only one they need, with the friendships and relationships developed in the circle lasting a lifetime.

On the other hand, working with any kind of group always requires compromise. You may want to do something the others don't, or vice versa. The personalities must click because the energy needs to flow freely. Everyone needs to socialize and be sociable. Differences of opinion as to beliefs or systems of practice need to be taken into consideration, which means they need to be overcome, ignored and forgotten, especially if you're entering an established group.

Groups usually have leaders, and sometimes an abundance of would-be leaders. Schisms often occur when a group becomes stagnant and self-complacent while some members are looking ahead and trying to learn new things. The field of knowledge evolves and expands, and when some in a group tend to fight this trend, a break-away group forms, made up of those who want more. Don't think that because a group is relatively new or can't lay claim to centuries of tradition it has no validity or is merely a bunch of self-involved, self-serving rebels who couldn't get along—they may provide the next great leap in our knowledge.

An existing group is going to have a set way of doing things. That's not bad if you're new and learning and if it works successfully for them, but it can be limiting. Too many people bypass reading, researching and personal investigation in favor of joining a group from the beginning and taking in everything they're taught without question. There are good working groups, good social groups, good working *and* social groups, as well as groups of nuts, crazies and sex maniacs. I strongly recommend that you learn some basics before getting involved with a group. The more you know and understand before jumping in, the better you'll be able to judge how suitable the group and its attitudes are for you. Any group that starts out by asking you too much about sex probably isn't going to teach you too much of any value.

If you do find an existing group that's been around for some time, is relatively stable, doesn't put undue emphasis during the interview on anything that leaves you feeling uncomfortable, isn't overly secretive (being careful is one thing, but if they're too secretive they're either hiding something they don't want you to know or they're overly paranoid, either of which is fair reason to stay away), and generally feels comfortable, by all means go ahead and give it a try. You need to keep experimenting, trying new things. If you feel at home with it, get along with its members, find nothing uncomfortable in its practices and they seem to be teaching you things that feel right to you, congratulations!

The Working Partner

Some people feel the best way to work is where one male and one female work together. (It can also be two men or two women and it would be better if they have opposite polarities, though that isn't really necessary.) This arrangement has its advantages. To begin with, two people working together will produce more than twice the energy of either one of you working alone, thus increasing the possibility of success in the operation. Secondly, your working partner is likely to be someone you're close to and comfortable with, so you'll be more open and you'll work more easily. Thirdly, together you probably would have the positive and negative forces of nature represented and working together. If the unity is present, the energy can flow between the two, building up until it's sent out. Finally, you simply can get more out of some things when you do them with someone else.

On the other hand, remember what was said about The Tie That Binds. The exchange and sharing of energies between two people causes changes in both of them—sometimes subtle, sometimes dramatic—and a link is formed between them that almost inevitably carries over into their everyday lives and frequently into their subsequent lives as well. The forming of this link can take some time and usually doesn't happen with one ritual, but it's something important to keep in mind before working with someone on a regular basis.

Polarity

Having both the positive and negative forces represented when two people are working partners is a concept that's comparatively easy to understand but not to use. It involves the matter of polarity. When discussing electricity, there are two polarities: negative and positive. The negative pole of a battery has a comparatively large number of excess electrons available versus the positive side. When the two are connected by a wire, electrons flow from the negative pole to the positive.

People are similar: some are negative and some are positive, and it has nothing to do with behavior or attitudes. It's energy. People who are predominantly negative have an easier time generating energy than those who are positive. Those who are positive generally have an easier time focusing energy. Energy flows from negative to positive. In working with a partner, the person most able to gather energy should do that and then feed it to the person better able to focus and direct it at the target of the work.

In a group utilizing a magick circle, usually a high priestess and high priest lead the group. They represent the goddess and god. The goddess is a symbol for the female, the moon, and the generative powers of the earth; the god represents the male, the sun, and the power it provides. You have both the female/male polarity and the power/focusing polarity, with the sun providing the energy and the earth utilizing it to produce life. See?

Generally, men are negative and women are positive, but there are plenty of positive men and negative women. Some people are bipolar, depending on the activity in which they're engaged and on their will. They can control their polarity by deliberate efforts. (This has nothing to do with being bisexual, homosexual, or anything else sexual.) So how can you tell who's what?

There's a fairly simple, if not totally dependable way of finding out. You start with the female-positive/male-negative assumption, then get someone of the opposite sex to do this little experiment with you: sit down comfortably across from each other and put your hands out, palms facing each other two to three inches apart. If one of you starts feeling warmer and the other starts feeling cooler in the palms, chances are you've got it nailed down—warmer from the energy coming in, positive; cooler from energy flowing out, negative. Doing this once isn't going to confirm it beyond a shadow of a doubt, nor is it going to allow for instances of bipolarity. If your palms almost always feel warm or cool with people of one sex and neutral with those of the other sex, there's little question. Conversely, if you almost always feel warm when working with a male and cool when working with a female, chances are you're naturally bipolar.

All magick depends on energy, and the more people you've got working together the more energy that's going to be available to put into the work. Polarity is important. Remember, energy flows, and the smoother the flow the better it is. If you have two people working together and one is positive while the other is negative, a natural flow can be established between them that makes the amount of available energy much greater. Usually if two people of the same polarity work together their energies will augment each other one-to-one, rather than providing a geometric increase: they're working in the same direction rather than truly working together. In terms of Wicca, it's preferable to have both polarities present as representatives of the goddess and god and the natural balance of the universe. (This is less true with ceremonial magick, since the goddess/god aspect is not being invoked.) If the ritual has a sexual aspect, having both partners of the same polarity makes the act superfluous.

Please keep all this in mind. It's important and often over-looked. Too often people assume that the man is going to be negative and the female is going to be positive. Not necessarily. And assumptions can get you into trouble when doing magick. In a Wiccan ritual where the individuals are taking representative roles, the positive partner is supposed to be the high priestess/goddess and the negative partner, of course, the high priest/god. If you've got a positive male and negative female, this could certainly cause some difficulties, as would having both partners of the same polarity. If that's the case, drop the role-playing. You can still do a simple worship ritual or magick ritual without taking on the roles of goddess/god. Besides, if you know you're the same polarity and you try to take on the roles of high priest and high priestess anyway, in the back of your mind you may be distracted by the feeling of the impropriety, and that will just detract from your work.

When two people work together the negative partner will gather the energy and feed it to the positive one. This individual should be concentrating only on the desired end result and leave the matter of getting the energy together to the negative partner. When more than two people work together, follow the same logical principle: someone ultimately is going to be responsible for gathering the energy and someone else for directing it. With two negative people and one positive, it's easy to choose roles. With two positives and one negative usually it's best to let one of the positives work with the negative to generate energy rather than risk having each positive put a different spin on the power as it's sent out.

With a larger group, you form the traditional circle, alternating positive/negative, join hands, and create a flow of energy around the circle. When the time is right the energy is released under the mental direction of the positive leader to do its work.

This is the basis of the coven: a group of people, lead by a high priestess (positive) and high priest (negative) as representatives of the goddess and god (positive and negative forces of nature), combining their energies in a geometric progression, working together for their mutual benefit and education.

Solo

Working solo has its advantages in that your activities are not constrained. You have no one to distract you, no one to tell you what to do and no one else to be concerned with. You have more flexibility because you can work in any manner you choose without being concerned with whether others will approve or be comfortable with it. You can do and say what you like in any manner you choose, leaving you free to experiment with anything you like. You have no one to shield yourself from, so maybe you'll be more open and able to concentrate better on what you want to do. You may have things you want to do but wouldn't do with others because of fear of their disapproval or lack of interest. You can work totally spontaneously. If you suddenly decide you want to do something, you can do it now, rather than have to take the time to call a group together, explain to them what you want to accomplish, and gain their cooperation.

Ceremonial magick is frequently performed solo. Since the magician is the center of focus in this form of magic and any others in the circle tend to be personal assistants rather than participants, working alone wouldn't seem to make that much difference. Since most of the magick performed in a Craft Circle involves a number of people, that's harder to perform solo. Such things as candle magick (also Craft) are usually done solo. Since most magick is mental to begin with, you can try anything you want to do solo, as long as you haven't become conditioned to associate certain acts with the presence of other people, in which case you might be fighting against yourself.

Working solo is good and necessary, particularly as it relates to the development of your imagination, concentration, ability to create and hold a visual image in your mind, center yourself, etc. However, you should not expect to be too successful in magickal workings while operating solo in the beginning. The benefits I outlined relating to working with a group are valid and having early successes because of the added energy of the group will do a lot more for your self-confidence and faith than a lot of early failures trying to working alone. If you develop enough of yourself, in time you should be fully capable of doing anything solo, magickally speaking, that you could do with a group.

The answer to whether you work alone or with others is always going to depend on your own inclinations. If you'd feel more comfortable with a group or can function uninhibitedly with others, by all means do so. If you wouldn't feel at ease with an existing group, but do have one or more people you can feel comfortable with, use that approach. Consider having a group of your own with everyone studying some different aspect of magic, psychism or occultism, then sharing it with the others so all of you are learning together. Whichever way you choose, always work solo, too. The more you practice the better you become. Do anything—a worship circle, a magickal work, prayers without a circle, whatever—on a regular basis to increase your abilities and your effectiveness. Practice makes perfect.

CHAPTER SEVEN

Getting Ready

WE CAN NOW BEGIN to look at the initial planning of a ritual. We'll first revisit the subject of the desired end result, then examine some of the terms we've been using—including the quarterpoints and their attributes—learn how to determine the best time to perform a given ritual and discuss how to use planetary correspondences.

The Desired End Result (Revisited)

In choosing your desired end result, keep one question in mind until the final decision is made: Is it worth it? To answer that question, you have to look at it in a lot of different ways. What's it going to do to you? Think about what you are, what you want to be and what you don't want to be. Think not only with your head, but also with your heart. What you do affects the way you think, particularly in magick.

The practice of magick will accentuate whatever aspect of your personality is the motivation for the rituals you do. Every personality has both a good and evil side to it, regardless of how well either is sublimated or consciously kept under control. If you decide to use a magick ritual to avenge yourself on someone for a wrong you feel has been done to you, you're going to be activating the negative aspects of your personality. The energy you put into that ritual is going to have an affect on your own personality in the process, stimulating and reinforcing the part that wants revenge and seeks to hurt people—the sadistic side. The more you call upon that side of your personality for your rituals, the stronger it will become and the more it will dominate your actions in all your relationships. You may look upon yourself as a good person and you may only want to avenge yourself this once for a particular wrong. Once may not be enough to do the job, but once may be enough to start changing you in ways you don't want to change.

Secondly, consider the possible long-term karmic effect. Ignoring a wrong will do more for you in the long run than taking revenge, which won't do much more than provide a temporary, short-term sense of satisfaction. You may feel that the sense of satisfaction is worth the risk, but in the end it really isn't.

In magick, everything has a price. While the karmic consideration is one aspect of this, it extends to present activities, too. Ideally, the price you pay for something is limited to the energy you put into it, but sometimes it can be a lot more than that, especially if you haven't mastered the art of protecting yourself. You must define your desired end result carefully in order to try to assure that you don't get it in a way you'd rather not have it. I know someone whose house got furnished through a friend's suicide, for instance.

The more positive the act, the less chance that anything negative will be involved as the price you end up paying. This isn't always the case, especially when attempting a healing using magick or even direct psychic intervention. If you can't or don't protect yourself, the imbalance created by countering the existing condition can result in your absorbing the forces that first created that condition. As an example, in the act of helping someone who has arthritis, you could develop arthritis yourself.

Since everything has a price, don't let yourself be the price. No matter how good your intentions, don't go so far as to say you're willing to take on the pain and suffering of another. First, you have no way of knowing if there's a karmic reason for the malady involved, so all you're going to accomplish is to delay the inevitable and temporarily deprive the individual of the opportunity to work out something. Secondly, such an act not only harms you now, but also sets up a karmic pattern that will need correcting later, so you'll end up paying the price twice for your actions. There's always more than one way to accomplish any desired end result, so look for the one that is most positive and has the least potential for hurting you (or someone else).

Let's go back to that idea of seeking revenge on someone for a wrong that was done to you. What is it you really want to accomplish? Your first answer may be along the lines of "To hurt them as they hurt me." Then you have to consider why they should be hurt. An answer might be "So they won't do it again." What you really want, then, is to teach them that they shouldn't cause harm to other people. Now you've turned a negative into a positive that can be approached in a more constructive manner.

Having redefined the desired end result, you can sit back and ponder that you're considering trying to teach them a lesson that they will learn eventually without your help. That may not solve the immediate problem or provide you with any personal satisfaction, but it's true. If that's not enough for you, look for other ways to achieve your goal without directly causing any harm. One possibility would be to set up an energy field around the person so that whenever the individual tried to harm another person it would backfire and end up causing something to happen to hurt them instead. An example of this would be to cause a burglar to slip up and leave some piece of evidence that would lead to an arrest. Another might be causing a bully to miss a blow, hit a wall and break his hand. This is not a matter of causing direct harm, but rather of setting up an if/then statement—if one thing happens, then something else specific happens.

Another reason for using the approach of turning a negative into a positive relates to the choice of entities called up in the ritual. A beneficent entity is easier to control/influence/cooperate with than a maleficent one. Also, the magickal operation is less apt to backfire on you or be fulfilled in an unpleasant way. In terms of planetary entities, you could certainly use the spirit of a planet to get back at someone, since it's the negative aspect of the planet, but it would be easier, safer and more effective to turn the negative into a positive and use the angel, instead. If you give enough thought to the problem you'll find some way to alter the destructive impulse into something positive that will achieve the same desired end result with less risk to yourself.

Next, let's get straightened out on some of the terminology we've been using.

Invocation v. Evocation

One of the dictionary definitions for invocation is "the act or process of petitioning for help or support." This suggests that any time you call upon a deity or other entity for help you are invoking that entity. Evocation is defined as "the act or fact of evoking: summoning as the summoning of a spirit." You could legitimately say one evokes in order to invoke. According to the dictionary, at least.

We're going to be more precise than that, turning to the derivations of the two words; "in" means within, "e" means without, and "voke" comes from the word meaning "to call." So if you invoke something, you are calling it to come into you, and if you evoke something you are calling it to appear outside of you. As examples, the ritual "Drawing Down the Moon" in Appendix D is a ritual of invocation, calling for the goddess to enter into the high priestess; all ceremonial rituals are evocations, calling for the entity to appear outside of the circle and specifically not to touch the magician.

Quarterpoints

Quarterpoint is the term used for the four cardinal points of the compass: north, south, east and west. Each is associated with a particular element and angel. Each element, in turn has its own properties, attributes and associations or "correspondences." In Appendix C you'll find a chart giving the names of the elements and their rulers, the angels, tarot suit, the ruling astrological sign, the sex and some of the qualities attributed to each. Each quarterpoint has an element, each element has its correspondences, and anything associated with a particular element can be used at its appropriate quarterpoint. Each element has both an invoking pentagram and a banishing pentagram that can be used to summon or banish an entity that is linked to the element. The banishing pentagram of Earth is the one used for general purposes, such as in the Lesser Banishing Ritual of the Pentagram.

Alternative schools of thought exist concerning the associations of the elements with the quarterpoints. For some, North is associated with air rather than earth, with earth placed in the East. Also, some use green for water in the West and blue is used for air. Let me try to explain the historical background for this and other kinds of associations.

All of the traditions we've discussed came from Europe or the Middle East. Fire is connected with the South since the sun is usually south of you if you're north of the equator. That's where heat comes from, giving you the association with red and fire. Likewise, with the Atlantic Ocean to the west, the element of Water was naturally placed there. Depending on where the people were living, predominant winds came from either the north or the east. That left Earth to the quarterpoint left over. If the traditions had developed on the East Coast of the U.S., things would probably have been very different with water in the East and air in the West.

Remember that it's important for you to be comfortable with the associations you have in your own mind as they relate to what you're doing. If you're standing on a beach watching the sun rise over the ocean, thinking of water to the west is going to seem silly.

The Planets and Correspondences

The use of planets and correspondences in magickal works is associated more with ceremonial magick than with Wicca, but even a Wiccan ritual can take advantage of the planetary correspondences that are intended to bring as much outside energy to bear on your work as possible. Each planet has certain attributes associated with it, and these attributes determine which planet is utilized in a ritual. The planet Mercury is associated with achieving "promptitude in business," for instance. For anything you want to do, there's a planet you would utilize for the ritual.

The correspondence refers to everything associated with a planet. In Appendix B you'll find the correspondences for day of the week, number, color, metal, sign of the zodiac, angel, archangel, spirit (negative), intelligence (positive), and herbs. Mercury, for example, is associated with the number 1, the color orange, the metal mercury, the zodiac signs of Gemini and Virgo, the angel Raphael, the archangel Michael, the spirit Taphtharth-arath, the intelligence Tiriel, and mandrake, lavender, hazel and other herbs and plants.

In preparing for your ritual you need to use as many of these as possible. In the case of Mercury, you would want to have an orange altar cloth inscribed with the appropriate signs and sigils. On it you'd set up your working tools along with one orange candle, some metallic mercury, and one or more of the herbs, both live and prepared as an incense (although the planetary oil may be preferable as the incense). Also, you should have a talisman (on either the proper metal or, lacking that, parchment) inscribed with the sigil of the entity you're going to evoke. The first time you do a ritual evoking a particular entity, it's probably best that you limit yourself to having the entity put its mark on the talisman, thereby endorsing it as a means of summoning the entity in the future. This is done by evoking the entity, showing it the talisman, informing it that the talisman is intended to be used for evoking it more quickly and easily in the future, request its agreement to that and tell it to put its mark on the talisman to seal the agreement. (Don't necessarily expect it to be visible to the naked eye, though.)

Having all of this on your altar is intended to create an environment conducive to the nature of the entity you're going to evoke: As Above, So Below. An entity is more likely to answer your call if you're surrounded with the plants and other elements that reflect its natural environment. This might sound a little ridiculous, but remember that *everything* has an energy field and things respond to fields most closely mimicking their own. For instance, an entity associated with the planet Mercury will be more aware of and responsive to the vibrational pattern around metallic mercury than to the pattern around copper. Likewise, when performing a ceremonial ritual, in the course of the evocation you draw the sigil of the entity in the air in front of you. The action of moving along that prescribed set of lines reactivates an ancient energy pattern inscribed on the astral plane that is recognizable to the entity whose sigil it is, resulting in an attraction of that entity. Always think in terms of the use of energy patterns and fields.

The attributes of the planets are usually associated with some observable aspect of the planet. Since Mercury is the fastest moving planet in our solar system, it's associated with communication and speed. Therefore, it's connected with such things as sports, promptitude, eloquence, answers, writings, merchandise (trade), and the color orange, which is itself representative of communication. The Moon affects the tides and rules the night, so you'd turn to the Moon's day, Monday, for things relating to contacting spirits, voyages, navigation and acquisition of merchandise by water. Jupiter is the largest planet and so is associated with abundance. It's all really quite logical. If you think about the nature of a planet or the mythical figure it's named after, you'll have a pretty good idea of what you can call on it for.

This last point can be especially helpful to remember when deciding which planet to use because sometimes you'll find more than one can be used for a particular purpose. Deciding between Mercury, the Moon, Saturn, Jupiter, or the Sun for instance, in matters of business, can depend on precisely what's involved. If you are trying to speed up a transaction or communication, then Mercury would be the best choice; for receiving a shipment from overseas you might find it better to use the Moon; for a real estate transaction you'd call on Saturn (good or bad fortune to buildings); for making a business grow and become larger, Jupiter would be the best selection; for obtaining the cooperation of others in a business deal the best choice would probably be the Sun.

Look at all the options and all the attributes of each planet in its full context before choosing. Consider the planet itself, its deity, and the other areas of influence before making a final choice.

The Day and Hour

Once you've decided which planet you want to work with, you have to determine when the best time is to perform the ritual. Each planet is associated with a specific day of the week in magick. This gives the entities associated with the planet a special emphasis on that particular day. All works that call upon an aspect of the planet's sphere of influence should be performed on the day of that planet. If you think about an attribute (such as writing) and find the appropriate planet for it (Mercury), you'll know on what day you need to perform your ritual (Wednesday).

Each planet also has an hour. Certain hours of each day are particularly conducive for working with each planet. Appendix B contains a table called "Hours of the Planets," but you should understand how this table is derived.

First, dawn of each day marks the first hour of the planet associated with that day. Second, the planets are traditionally listed in a specific order, reflected in the number of each planet, as follows: Mercury, Moon, Saturn, Jupiter, Mars, Sun, Venus. So the first hour of Wednesday, beginning at dawn, is the hour of Mercury, the second hour is the hour of the Moon, the third hour is the hour of Saturn, and so on. After the seventh hour (Venus), the cycle repeats itself, making the eighth hour of Wednesday also the hour of Mercury.

However, we're not dealing with 60-minute hours here. There are 12 hours each of day and night for magickal purposes and only at the equinox, plus or minus a few days depending on where you live, are the planetary hours 60 minutes long. To find the proper clock time for a ritual you need to decide first if you're going to perform your ritual in the day or at night. Most people find night preferable since it doesn't interfere with showing up for work, concentration is often easier and there are fewer outside energies causing interference. If you decide to do it at night, check a newspaper or the TV weather report to find out when the sun will set that night and rise the next morning. Next, calculate how long the night is in terms of hours and minutes from sunset to sunrise, convert the hours to minutes by multiplying by 60, add that number to the number of minutes, then divide the total by 12 to obtain the length of the planetary hour for the night.

For example, let's say that sunset is at 8:52 P.M. and sunrise will be at 6:28 A.M. That makes the night 9 hours 36 minutes long. Multiplying 9 by 60 equals 540 minutes; add 36 and you have 576 minutes. Dividing 576 by 12 tells us that each planetary hour will be 48 minutes long. Sunset marks the first hour of the night, which on Wednesday would be the hour of the sun. Looking at the table, the second hour would be the hour of Venus and it would start at 9:40 (8:52 plus :48). The third hour, the hour of Mercury, would begin at 10:28 (9:40 plus :48) and run until 11:16 P.M. Any planetary hour of the day or night can be calculated in this manner. Hours of the day would be calculated from sunrise to sunset, so with the above times each planetary hour would be 72 minutes long.

You'll notice from the table that each planet appears four times on its day, so you have a choice of times to start your ritual. The first, obviously, is dawn (6:28 A.M. in this case) since this starts the day; the second time would be at 2:52 P.M. based on the 72-minute hour we calculated; the third is at 10:28 P.M. and the fourth, which you might think precedes these, being at 12:52 A.M. (since we tend to think of anything after midnight as being a new day), actually would be at 4:04 A.M. on Thursday, because a day begins and ends at dawn, not midnight.

A ritual can be started in any of those four planetary hours. While you may begin a ritual any time within the appropriate hour—say between 10:28 and 11:16 P.M.—it's preferable to begin and end within that same time period if you're doing a working ritual rather than practicing or using it to obtain information. It's not essential that you end within the planetary hour, it's just preferable. Never let yourself feel rushed. If you start at the beginning of the hour and you know what you're doing, you can complete any ritual within the planetary hour, regardless of how short that hour may be.

All of the above discussion is a matter of the best or most suitable time to perform your ritual. You'll notice there are attributes assigned as "In the Hour" of the planet which usually reflect some of the attributes of "On the Day." Performing a ritual in the hour of Mercury on Wednesday is preferable to performing it in the hour of Mercury on Monday, for instance, but you could still do it on Monday. It would take more work than doing it on Wednesday, but there may be cases when time is of the essence and you can't wait for the appropriate day. If that's the case, do your work in the hour of the planet on whatever day you have to do it, or re-examine your approach to the problem so you can put it into terms that fit an earlier day. If you feel there's something you'd best address on Wednesday, but you can't wait that long and it seems that Monday is close enough in its aspects so as to be a reasonable substitute, then do it in the hour of the Moon on Monday.

You can perform a given ritual in the appropriate hour of the appropriate day, anytime during the day, any day at the appropriate hour, or change the ritual to suit the day and/or hour when you're able to do it. The first option is the best choice and the last option is the least desirable. Your decision will rest on a combination of circumstances and your own patience.

The foregoing is technically sufficient for deciding when to perform a ritual. The following additional aspects relating to timing are intended to bring more energies to bear on your behalf and to make things more beneficial in general.

Other Planetary Aspects

You should consider the phase of the moon when planning your ritual. The principle is to use the waxing moon (between new and full) for beneficial works and anything related to increasing something, and the waning moon (between full and new) for negative works and anything related to decreasing something. In Wicca, the full moon and new moon are not times for magickal works, and are used only for worship rituals. Others consider these to be the two most powerful times and use them liberally. As with picking a day or an hour for the ritual, rethinking your approach can usually change a desired end result from increasing to decreasing in nature, or vice versa, making the current phase of the moon appropriate for your goals.

Sticking with Mercury for examples, if you wanted to speed up the closing of a business deal and you wanted to use Mercury, you could use the waxing moon for increasing the speed at which the deal is considered and closed. If you're in a waning moon, you might think in terms of decreasing procrastination or resistance. If the reversal adds a negative aspect to the work itself, you might be better off waiting for the proper phase.

The location of the planet in the zodiac will also have some bearing. Mercury's zodiac correspondences are both Gemini and Virgo. If you can wait until Mercury is located within one of those signs, it will strengthen the Mercurial aspects you're bringing into play in your ritual. If you're not already into astrology, it wouldn't be a bad idea to study it. In the meantime, you can buy publications that can give you this information, such as *The Witches' Almanac* and various Craft-oriented calendars, and even *The Old Farmer's Almanac*.

Another aspect involves the nature of the work you're doing. You'll see that under the day of Mercury is ". . . converse with spirits (especially when moon is in an air sign)." The idea is that spirits are airy in nature, so having Mercury (communications) in an air sign (such as Aquarius) would be beneficial to that particular work.

Astrologically, those are the bare-bone basics. If you study
astrology, you'll come to understand the relationships of planets
to each other and to particular houses of the zodiac, after which
you'll be able to determine for yourself the optimal time for
performing any given ritual. As I said earlier, this isn't essential
for doing a ritual, but every little bit helps, and someday you may
find yourself involved with something requiring special attention
and every positive aspect you can possibly have working for you.

The Entity

Having determined when you should perform a ritual, you need
to consider who/what you're going to evoke/invoke for that ritual.
Since each quarterpoint has an entity associated with it, those
entities will be evoked for protective purposes, whether you're
doing a Wiccan or ceremonial ritual. If you're doing the moon
ritual mentioned for conversing with spirits, you'll probably want
to evoke Paralda, King of Air, in particular at the quarterpoints.
If you're performing a Wiccan ceremony, obviously the applicable
goddess and/or god is going to be invoked for the ritual, after
which (if appropriate) you might call upon some other deity in
the pantheon in the name of the goddess or god. Using the
Egyptian tradition, perhaps you'd initially invoke Isis or Ra, and
then evoke Sahkmet if her attributes were more in keeping with
the work you've got in mind.

There is another side to this, though. While there is an
entity/goddess/god/angel/archangel best suited to any particular
work, it's also true that you are doing the work, so consider
personal compatibility, also. For instance, let's assume you feel
more comfortable with an Egyptian atmosphere than a Celtic
one; most of your rituals will call on elements of the Egyptian
pantheon to help you. Next, let's say that for a particular work
it would be best (theoretically) to call on Sahkmet, but you don't
really feel comfortable with her. On the other hand, maybe you

have a very definite personal affinity for Hathor—you can relate
to her, feel close to her, and share many personality traits with
her. Under those circumstances try working with Hathor before
you turn to Sahkmet. Think of it in terms of turning to a friend
for help before turning to a stranger. Most deities have more than
one side to their personalities, just as humans do. Even Aphrodite
was capable of vengence, for instance, and if you naturally feel
a close kinship with her but abhor Aries/Mars, then ask your
friend for help and turn to the stranger as a last resort. Remember:
if you don't feel comfortable with what you're doing it's not going
to work for you.

In ceremonial, the best approach in the beginning is to use
the lowest level entity available. After all, there's no sense going
to the president of the company for help if a line-worker can do the
job. If you've got a really difficult problem, evoke the archangel,
otherwise use the angel. If you have a comparatively minor problem, then the intelligence should be sufficient. The lower the
order of the entity, the easier it is to summon and the easier to
obtain cooperation. For any kind of negative work, you're better
off using the spirit of the planet rather than any of the other
three.

A simple principle is at work in all of this: keep the demands
on yourself as low as possible. The more power you can evoke
through proper timing and the preliminary evocations of lower
orders (such as elementals), the less energy you will have to
expend in the course of the ritual itself. The less energy you have
to expend yourself, the more likely you will be successful in your
work. Conversely, if you try to evoke the wrong entity on the
wrong day at the wrong hour, you might as well chalk up the
whole thing as a waste of time. Even if it does appear (which is
unlikely), there won't be a thing it can do for you. Remember
that.

CHAPTER EIGHT

The Circle, Tools and Supplies

THIS CHAPTER DEALS WITH the physical structure of a magick ritual: the circle and the things that go into it. These items include the altar itself, the altar cloth, candles, incense (and burner), athame, wand, salt, water, and various miscellaneous items of choice.

Specific steps are incorporated into virtually every magick ritual that utilizes a circle. You begin with a consecration and purification of the area in which you're going to work, consecration of the ritual elements of earth, fire and water, then the formation of the circle itself. This is sometimes followed by summoning the Lords of the Watchtowers, the rulers of each element. Next is the invocation of the deity, if appropriate, the building of your power, the evocation of the appropriate spirit, the request/command, the license to depart for the spirit, and the closing of the circle with the final purification of the area and storing of the circle.

The casting of the circle is the setting-apart of the ritual place as a special area apart from the rest of the world. In *every* magickal ritual, whether of medieval Europe, present day America or Africa of 2000 B.C.—whatever the place or time—special attention is paid to the place of worship and magickal workings. Whether you cast a circle, an oval, a square or a trapezoid, the sacred spot is always set apart from the rest of the world and made holy and potent. If any grimoire (book of magick rituals) you're using doesn't specify using something like a circle for protection, *do it anyway.*

Why would you do something if it's not called for in the book? For one thing, you may need the protection. For another thing, some books intentionally contain false information on the theory that anyone "worthy" enough to perform the work will know what's right and how to correct the ritual while those who shouldn't be doing it won't be able to because of the misleading information. It is generally assumed you have certain basic knowledge and don't *need* to be told certain things. For instance, you're expected to know that you need to do a circle for protection and you don't have to be told how to do one.

The first step is usually the purification of the area itself. I'm recommending that the Lesser Banishing Ritual of the Pentagram (LBR) be used for this. You don't have to use the LBR, of course, but it makes for a good all around banishing ritual to clean up the room. Once the room is cleaned, you can consecrate the elements and use them to define the circle itself.

Then you need to invoke the powers. Whether you perceive this power to be the Christian God, a pagan god(dess), an angel, or your own spiritual self isn't important. You have to draw the power from somewhere and fill yourself with it. In the LBR, for instance, this is done by picturing the six-rayed star shining over you and sending its power down through your spine ("the column") to electrify your body. In some martial arts systems this power is called ch'i. In yogic systems it is kundalini. In Polynesia, mana. In some Nordic traditions, vril. It's pictured as a lightning bolt or as a serpent, emphasizing its spiral, twisting nature and its speed.

Although the invocation is a verbal invocation, prayer, or even command, a subtle change must occur within the body as well. The operator is summoning up his psychic strength. In Voodoo this is done with the rhythm of the drums. In the Craft it's done by forming a circle with the high priestess in the center, and then dancing and chanting or singing. Power also can be raised through raising your consciousness by assuming a god-form, meaning identifying yourself with a power source such as Horus, Osiris, Zeus, Odin, Ahura-Mazda, Isis, Diana, Cerridwen, Freya, etc. By using something along the lines of Drawing Down the Moon, which we get to in the next chapter, you invoke the deity into yourself and/or working partner.

The main body of the ritual comes next. Whether your're evoking a planetary entity, charging a talisman, consecrating your working tools or anything else, this is where the work comes in. In closing you'll thank those you've deliberately called upon— everything from beginning to end—for their help, protection, guidance, and then dissolve the circle.

Finally, do another LBR or other banishing until you're certain your place is clean again. Banish whatever you called up (unless it's a familiar you've been creating or an elemental spirit you need for a specific piece of work; if it's an elemental, you need to set a time for it to die and then kill it.) But *always*, *always*, banish everything that may be around the circle when you're through with it. You may not be aware of other things that have been called up or attracted by your efforts and you can't take any chances. Don't bet your life on your level of sensitivity. *Banish!*

Whenever you see a ritual, look for these steps. If all you have is some conjurations and names of spirits you should know enough to add the rest of the ritual yourself. Don't just stand there in the middle of the room reading a conjuration. The results might not be too pleasant.

The Circle

The circle is the area in which you work. It's both a physical area and a mental area because it is set apart from everything else in all respects. When you cast the circle, you're creating a kind of separate universe—apart from the normal, everyday physical world—in which you work with the powers and energies of other worlds. Think of it, perhaps, as a kind of way station between worlds that contains elements of both, is part of neither, and can serve as a meeting ground for all parties involved or invited. To paraphrase the consecration itself, the circle is a "place that is not a place . . . a time that is not a time . . . on a day that is not a day . . . between the worlds and beyond."

This may sound a little corny, but as with so much else, it's a matter of the psychology of the thing. The circle is not just another part of the room, not by a long shot. Properly created and maintained, it has some definite characteristics you won't find in other places. The circle is created for two reasons: to keep the energy you want to use in (and concentrated) while keeping the energy (or entities) you don't want out. It's a very real boundary, formed of your own energy.

Let's take these two aspects one at a time. In casting the circle, you'll actually be creating an energy field around your working area, and consecrating it using the traditional four elements of earth, air, fire and water. When I say you here, I mean you individually or all of you in the group. As you build up energy during the ritual itself, you don't hold all that energy inside yourself. Some is released, especially if there's a group utilizing singing, chanting and/or dancing, and gathered in the circle. That energy can be utilized in your work and the circle helps to keep it close at hand.

From a distance outside the circle you can sometimes see what looks like a white cone rising into the sky from the circle with the circle itself providing the actual ground-based boundary. That's the Cone of Power. It's composed of all the energy that's been gathered and generated, released into the circle and confined there. Like the human aura, the more sensitive you are the easier it is to see, but it's always there. When the ritual is reaching its conclusion and you're ready to release all the energy you've built up and direct it to your desired end result, that energy first is released into your circle where it joins with the energy contained in the cone before going out to do its job. At that point, the sensitive, outside observer would see the cone rise into the air and, depending on the direction it was given, bend and extend itself off into the distance.

The second purpose of the circle is keeping the energy (or entities) you don't want out. This point has a number of different aspects to it. First, there are simply some negative places. Every place in the world where there are people you'll find residues of the presence of those people. That's why some places feel good to us and some feel bad. Good places have generally had positive people around and/or good things have occurred there. A lot of positive energy is left in the place and we can feel it, consciously or subconsciously. The same can be said of bad places. These places have experienced a lot of violence, hate or depression. A lot of negative emotions were released in such places and that, too, can affect us.

The physical circle is looked upon as a place for magick and power, and for some as a place of worship. The "petty" elements of the outside world shouldn't have a place in it. When you're casting the circle, all of your attention should be on what you're doing and nothing else. In setting aside this particular area for your magick work, you should be setting it aside in your mind, too. Nothing else should enter into it. Though you'll often hear of how the magick circle is intended to keep demons out, that's partly symbolic—demons come in many forms. If you bring in the outside world—if your thoughts are distracted by problems at work or a big date Saturday or where you're going to get the money to pay the rent—obviously you're not going to be concentrating your full attention on the work at hand. When you put up your circle, think of yourself as being in another world where nothing matters except what's going on right at that moment. Leave your personal demons outside.

When doing a ritual keep in mind that any energies around you can affect the quality of your work and that while performing the ritual you're opening yourself up to anything around you. The sensitivity you want to develop in yourself can leave you vulnerable if you're not careful. You'll naturally tune in to whatever's around you. If you're in a place with a lot of negative energy, that energy can affect you unless you protect yourself. The circle will help to serve that purpose. Just as it helps to confine the energy you're generating during the ritual, it also helps keep out any uninvited energies that may be around the place itself.

The next point concerns other entities. While performing your ritual, you may call upon someone or something to help you. That's fine, unless what you're calling upon isn't, strictly speaking, beneficent. I know that some of you will try your hand at playing with a demon or two at some time in your future. I wouldn't stop you, but I would remind you that you're probably going to be open and vulnerable if you're doing your ritual properly, and if you're not properly protected, you may be truly sorry later on. (See *The Secrets of Dr. Taverner* by Dion Fortune[10] for some insight into the connection between psychic sensitivity and insanity.)

You will also attract other things simply by virtue of doing psychic or magickal work. Ghosts, elementals, and various other entities are sensitive to the kind of energy you'll be giving off. (As a matter of fact, in time you'll start to notice that things seem to come into the room when you just have conversations on the subject. Usually, in such cases, they're just curious and drawn by your energy; sometimes they'll be of significantly higher intellect and want to know what's going on or even have some input into the discussion. You normally don't have to concern yourself with them, just go on with your conversation.) You don't want these things getting in your way. While the circle itself may attract some things to the physical area, it will still keep them away from you.

The circle is there to isolate you, protect you and help you all at the same time. Why a circle? Practically speaking, it's easy, convenient and the strongest form of its kind. Think of a circle

---

[10]Dion Fortune, *The Secrets of Dr. Taverner* (St. Paul, MN: Llewellyn Publications, 1979).

compared to a square: the square has joints that can be weak points; the circle is a continuous line with no specific weak points. Symbolically, the circle is eternity, the unity of the universe, god (as in no beginning and no ending), and various other things that you can look up elsewhere, should the spirit move you.

The circle is usually nine feet in diameter. A circle that large can comfortably accommodate a number of people at the same time while keeping them close together. Some take the position that any diameter that's a multiple of three feet— six, nine or twelve—is okay.

Other traditions take different approaches. Some instruct that a cignuluum be worn by the people in the circle. This is a cord constructed by taking three lengths of cord, each one nine feet long, and braiding them together. One use for this is to pin one end in the center of the circle, then use the other end to define the perimeter of the circle. The circle will vary in diameter according to how tightly the individual has braided those three lengths of cord.

While a circle is the ideal, you don't have to be too much of a stickler for the precise shape, just as the traditional diameter of nine feet isn't necessarily cast in stone. If the most suitable place for the ritual is your living room and you don't feel inclined to move the sofa, stereo and TV in order to get a perfectly round nine-foot circle, you don't have to. If it comes out as an oval of five feet by seven feet, that's okay. A six-foot circle would be better, but the oval is acceptable as long as you can work within its boundaries. For the sake of this book, we'll assume you've got a circle and leave it at that.

The physical depiction of the circle on the floor is not necessary. Desirable, maybe, but not necessary. The heart of the circle is the energy you put into it. Using chalk, crayon, or paint to draw it on the floor has some advantages, but it can be dispensed with.

First you must decide just where the circle is going to be. When you put energy into something, regardless of what it is, a residue will remain when you're finished. Sometimes this is something you'll actually desire, as with the circle, so put the circle in a place you can use repeatedly. Many people dedicate a separate room only for their magickal work, but in any event you'll want to define an area that will be easy to use, of sufficient size, and one that you can retrace in the future without having to stop to remember where it was last time. That's an advantage to physically drawing the circle on the floor.

On the negative side, if you're using your living room or some other area to which other people have access, they might not be too understanding, so you'll need to conceal the drawing. Some people I've known have purchased large rugs or carpets to put on the floor that can be rolled up out of the way while they're working. I also have an aesthetic problem with this approach. The prospect of having a lop-sided, mutated egg-shaped drawing staring me in the face is not attractive. Seeing the bluish-white light of such a form during a ritual is one thing, seeing it drawn on the floor in physical reality is something else. On the other hand, if I had the space available and convenient, I very well might go with a permanent perfect circle on the floor.

You've decided to have your circle, oval or whatever on the floor in a permanent place. I'd suggest you do it in white—a nice, neutral, safe color. You can do it in black, too, but I'd stay away from using any other color for a permanent circle because of the associations colors have with different types of work. Just as we assumed your circle is a circle, we're also going to assume it's white and nine feet in diameter. That's all there is to your basic circle. There can be more, but that's all you really need.

Beyond the basic circle itself, the most common element added is the pentagram. A lot of people use it and it doesn't necessarily denote any particular attitude, belief, school or tradition. The pentagram is used by everyone for something because of its symbolism of the four elements plus spirit. If you want to draw a pentagram within your circle, go ahead and do so. Literally dozens of different designs can appear as part of the circle above and beyond just the pentagram.

A common starting point is a second circle encompassing the first one about one foot away from it. Into that space you put additional designs or names. Some people will put various names of god within this space. Others will put the names of the angels associated with the appropriate quarterpoint and others will put the names of the ruler of the element of that quarterpoint. Some do it in English while others use Hebrew or Latin. Some will add the symbol of a planet associated with that direction or element at the moment. For instance, the sun may be in Leo at the time. Leo's a fire sign, so the symbol for Leo would be put in the South. If you're doing a Jupiter ritual and Jupiter is in the east at that time, then the symbol for Jupiter would be written to the east of the circle. On the other hand, some would write the name of the archangel, angel, spirit and intelligence of Jupiter into the circle to accent the concept of the work being associated with that planet.

The possibilities are endless, and they're important if you're doing a ceremonial ritual. The creation of the symbols and the energy that becomes part of them in the course of the ritual give them a kind of life, so you need to use symbols that are historically associated with the work you want to attempt, make sure they're appropriate and exact, and make sure they go together as a unit. Some are connected with the quarterpoint itself, others change depending on the work being done at the time. There should be a consistency of purpose behind them; they can't be chosen simply because they look interesting.

If you're going to draw anything permanent, stick to generalities. Don't start drawing anything related to changing astrological/astronomical conditions. If using names, try using the Hebrew letters because of the long historical precedent for this approach. (Remember: precedent does count for something.)

One final note on this subject. Drawing a circle on the floor, with or without the outer circle, names, symbols, etc., is not a substitute for creating the circle psychically each time you do a ritual. Your energy creates the circle, not the chalk or paint. In time the permanent circle probably will retain a permanent charge because of what you've put into it, but don't use that as an excuse to avoid starting from scratch each time.

The Triangle

The triangle is of concern only to those who use the ceremonial approach. You locate the triangle outside of your circle as the place wherein whatever you call up is to appear. As a symbol of the Trinity, the triangle is said to have the power to contain any entity you summon, though I'd caution you to be selective on that subject in the beginning. No symbol you draw, construct or utilize in any other fashion will be *inherently* powerful enough to protect you. If you're evoking an entity, make sure you specify that it enter the triangle, but don't trust the triangle to protect you all by itself. Ultimately, only your own knowledge, experience and power will do that.

The Altar

The altar goes near the center of the circle, usually facing east. Some put it so they're facing north, others facing the direction of the sun at the particular hour they're working, but most set it up facing east. The exact positioning is usually dependent upon the size of the circle. If possible, it should allow you to stand at the center.

You can use about anything for the altar that gives you enough room and is a comfortable height. Some people use a coffee table or TV stand. Wood is good. A glass top is nice. Try to avoid metal if at all possible. It should be able to hold anything and everything you want to use in a ritual and you should be able to reach everything without continually stooping down. Waist high is generally a good rule of thumb for the height.

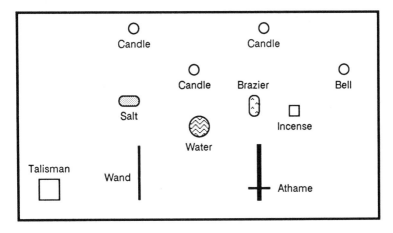

Figure 1. Basic altar arrangements.

What does it need to hold? The basics common to all rituals are two white candles, incense, something to burn the incense in, a bowl of salt, a glass or chalice of water, and your athame. Sometimes you'll have additional candles, a wand, maybe a bell, perhaps some piece of metal and/or flowers associated with the particular work you're planning to do, an appropriate crystal or gem, a picture or something belonging to an individual if the magick is to be directed at someone in particular, and maybe a piece of parchment (or paper) with a sigil on it. (See figure 1.) In other words, you'll add to the basics anything available that is associated with the planet you've chosen to work under or the person you've chosen to work on, or both.

The Altar Cloth

Usually, but not necessarily always, you'll have an altar cloth. White's fine, but if you're doing a specific work of magick you should have an altar cloth of the appropriate color. If you're doing a Mercury ritual, for instance, use orange. (The table of correspondences in Appendix B will give you all the colors.) These can be made of cloth or, in a pinch, look for a paper tablecloth in a store that has birthday party supplies.

The altar cloth may have things drawn on it or it may be plain. Drawings can include such things as a pentagram, and anything associated with the appropriate planet, such as the symbol for the planet, the sigil of its rulers, or the astrological sign it's in at the moment. If you're doing a money ritual, you might want to cover the altar cloth with a lot of monetary symbols such as $$$$$, £££££, ~~YYYYY~~, or whatever. For a love ritual you might write your target's name all over it with a lot of hearts. You can draw anything symbolic of what you want to do or what you want to work with.

Candles

In Wiccan or pagan rituals there will always be at least three candles on the altar, two represent the goddess and god and the third is used to light everything else. They're lit at the beginning of the ritual and stay lit throughout. Candles are almost never *blown* out. Either use a candle-snuffer or your bare (unwetted) finger. Candles relating to the planetary correspondence can (and should) also be used on the altar. You can use one or a number relating to the number of the planetary power being evoked.

You'll also need quarterpoint candles. These usually are larger candles, always solid in color, with the color corresponding to the color appropriate to that quarterpoint. You'll need at least one each of yellow, red, blue and green.

Aside from the goddess/god candles, planetary candles (if being used) and quarterpoint candles, you'll need to have a significant supply of other candles in stock for use in candle magick. I'll get into that subject in a little more detail later, but for now think of making a wish on a birthday cake's candles as being a form of candle magick.

The candles can be bought from a store or you can hand-dip your own. In either case, make sure they're solid in color rather than white candles dipped in a color for the outside surface. Also, make sure they're unscented, unless you're making your own and add a scent associated with the planet. If you are making your own, it could work to your advantage to make them within a circle during the appropriate hour on the appropriate day. Preparing everything you can within the confines of a circle helps to assure the purity of the object.

Now let me explain more about the quarterpoints.

Quarterpoints

The quarterpoints are the four cardinal points of the compass: east, south, west and north, usually according to the sun rather than the compass. Marking them for the circle can be a little awkward in practice because: (a) some city people don't get to see the sun much from inside their homes; (b) the sun is always in motion relative to the earth, rising in the same place only twice in a year; (c) using the point of sunrise as the East and sunset as the West will not yield a perfect circle. Do the best you can. Use a compass if you have to in order to locate the quarterpoints, but always try to get as close as possible to the sunrise-sunset axis for east-west.

The quarterpoints are marked physically by the quarterpoint candles. These are the large candles mentioned earlier: for East, the direction of the sunrise, a yellow candle is used; at the South quarterpoint, use red for fire; for West, blue, water; for North, green, earth. Some people also like to put symbols of the elements at the quarterpoints, using a small bell (preferably glass) at the East quarterpoint (using the association of sound with air), a second candle to the south, a small bowl of water for West and a second small bowl or dish containing either salt or some soil as the earth for the North. Since the rim of the circle will fall immediately outside the quarterpoint candles, if you use these elemental symbols they should be placed to the inside of the candles where they can be reached without crossing the circle.

Incense and Brazier

Incense is used in almost everything you do. In both religious and magickal circles, incense is used in casting the circle and in adding atmosphere to what you're doing. In magickal work, different end results are associated with different planets, and each planet has a different sort of incense associated with it.

The form of the incense depends only on what's available— not only what you can buy or make, but also what you can burn it in. For instance, sticks, cones and cubes are the most commonly found forms in which you'll find incense, and small burners can easily be purchased in which to burn them. Occult and religious supply houses sell a wide range of incenses. If one of these places isn't readily available to you, most of them will sell by mail. On the other hand, the supermarket also can be a convenient source of incenses. Examples of what can be found there include thyme, cinnamon, cloves, just about any herbal spice, tobacco, and camphor. (Be careful of the camphor—that's mothballs—a little goes a long way and too much will make the room totally uninhabitable for a long time!) One drawback to the pre-packaged herbs in supermarkets is their lack of freshness. What is acceptable for cooking may not be totally acceptable as an incense. For this application you want the freshest ingredients you can obtain.

Natural incenses, rather than those that are pre-prepared and pre-formed, you burn on charcoal. Stores that sell incenses usually will have a kind of flat, self-starting charcoal specially made for this application. You light the charcoal, get it going well, then pour your incense on top of it. Remember, it will burn very quickly so the room will fill up fast with smoke if you put too much on at once, and you will be putting the incense to the fire fairly frequently throughout the ritual. I say this as a warning on how to use it, not to put you off using this form of incense. It's generally accepted that the natural form on charcoal is preferable to the pre-processed sticks, cones and such. (Remember to disconnect any smoke alarms beforehand. Firemen breaking down your door with axes might distract you from your work.)

Incenses can be mixed, also. When doing a Jupiter or Venus ritual, you may want to use more than one of the incenses associated with the planet. The tables of correspondences in Appendix B will give you some of the incenses associated with each planet. Feel free to mix and match within each planet's listing as you see fit, and according to what smells best to you. Also, you can obtain a copy of *Culpeper's Herbal*[11] for a more complete, traditional listing.

If you can't find what you need for a particular ritual, use your own common sense and intuition. For a love ritual, you'll want something of a sweet-smelling nature. On the other hand, a ritual for revenge will call for something with a strong, unpleasant odor. Guidelines are plentiful; hard and fast rules are rare. If you don't have what you are supposed to have, improvise. Use something that feels right to you and have faith in your own intelligence and intuition.

It's virtually always proper, and sometimes preferable, to use oils as incense. Basically, these are extracts of herbs, flowers, woods, etc., in a pure oil base. The oil can have a number of applications, but the one we're concerned with at the moment is burning as incense. You use it just like the solid forms we've talked about, but it's concentrated so a little goes a very long way. You may find cases in which an angel, elemental, or some other entity you call up informs you in no uncertain terms that it wants you to use an oil instead of the solid form. Do it.

As far as the brazier is concerned, you can burn your incense or oil in almost anything. Something along the lines of a small

---

[11]Nicholas Culpeper, *Culpeper's Complete Herbal* (Cedar Knolls, NJ: Wehman Bros., 1960).

caldron is nice. Lacking that, a bowl or dish with some dirt or sand in the bottom will certainly do. The only thing you need to keep in mind is that you'll be carrying it around the circle so it needs to be something you can carry easily, without getting burned, and if you're using cones or sticks, something that will not drop or spill the incense.

Athame

The athame (ATH-uh-may or sometimes uh-THA-me) is the most-used tool you'll work with. It's a black-handled knife with a blade six to eight inches long, maximum. In the ritual it's used to define the circle, consecrate the elements, and is itself a symbol for the element of air.

In the old days everything witches worked with had to look like a normal, everyday household article to avoid being tortured and burned; a simple cutting knife with a black handle would not attract attention. Today there's a little more privacy, if not necessarily more tolerance, so the athame may be inscribed with various signs, symbols or words, many utilizing one of the many mystic alphabets such as runic.

The athame, once consecrated (like all working tools), is an extension of yourself. It's used to define the boundaries of the circle, to consecrate other items used either on a permanent basis or for a particular ritual, to salute, and to magickally defend the individual from attack. The athame is used more often, for more things, than any other single tool. One thing it's *not* used for is cutting. Think of the athame as being used inside the circle in matters pertaining to other planes—consecrations, commanding spirits, etc.—not for mundane things like cutting herbs nor for inscribing things used in the circle.

In choosing a knife for your athame, it doesn't matter what the knife was originally intended for. It could be a kitchen knife, a hunting knife, a decorative knife or anything else. The important thing is that it must feel right to you. Once you start using a knife as your athame you don't use it for anything else anymore.

It's often said that, like the Craft, the athame chooses the individual rather than vice versa. You may be walking down the street, window shopping for something, when suddenly you'll see a knife in a window that stands out to you. It may not have a black handle when you see it, but you'll know that's the knife you want. If the handle isn't black you can always replace it or paint over it.

One last important point about the athame: don't feel as though you must do without until it finds you. You may use any black-handled knife available that you can consecrate until you find that one, special knife you want as your permanent athame. Also, you can change athames. One day you may see a knife you like even more than the one you're already using. If so, deconsecrate the athame you have and consecrate the new one.

Other Blades

The *kerfan* is a white-handled knife that serves as the earthly counterpart to the black-handled athame. While the athame is used for other-plane matters, the kerfan is used within the circle for all things involving cutting, carving, or inscribing things (such as candles).

The *boleen*, on the other hand, is used for cutting outside of the circle. If you decide to pick your own herbs to use as incense for a ritual, the boleen is what you'd use for doing the cutting.

The *sword* is largely treated the same as the athame, but is more commonly found in ceremonial rituals than in pagan ones. There's no prescribed length for the blade, but the general rule is to keep it down to something manageable. Having a long, broad sword might seem like fun, but once you get it into a circle you may find it to be unwieldly, awkward, and generally dangerous.

Wand

You use the sword and athame in command-type situations where it's necessary to order cooperation of a spirit. When it's preferable to request or coax cooperation, you generally use the wand. The wand is used in many cases like the athame and, in fact, some people treat it as the primary tool and rarely use the athame at all. A basic rule of thumb is to use the wand in the course of the ritual itself (not counting the casting of the circle) when you don't want to threaten. If the ritual involves commanding something to obey you, then use the athame; if the ritual involves entreating the aid of something, use the wand.

So many different ideas exist on the preparation of the wand that it would take an entire chapter to list them all. To keep it simple, take about 18"–24" of oak or willow, remove the bark, smooth the knots from it, then put something on or in the end. That something could be a silver cap, or a quartz crystal (both associated with energy) or a small piece of cotton or linen and insert it in the end with a couple of drops of your blood on it.

It's becoming popular to combine crystals with the wand by making a wand of wood or glass and either inserting crystals directly into it or working a piece of metal (preferably silver) into a vine design around the wand and setting the crystals into that. One might create a wand containing all the crystals related to controlling energy, or have a series of wands for different magickal applications such as healing rituals, love rituals, etc. This can become an expensive proposition, because aside from the expense of good books on the nature of crystals, the stones themselves aren't cheap.

Salt

Salt for the ritual is placed into a small dish on the altar and can also be placed at the North quarterpoint. Use natural sea salt, not iodized. The salt plays two roles in the ritual. First, it's a symbol for the element of earth, which is why it's placed at the North quarterpoint (or East, as the case may be). Second, it is a consecration element used to cast the circle.

Salt is a protective element. As the ritual for the consecration of salt puts it, ". . . as water purifies the body, so doth salt purify the soul," that puts it in the category of a spiritual plane protector. It's used not only for casting the circle, but also as a general protective measure in other things not necessitating a circle. Salt is often put into the corners of a room to help cleanse it and protect it from negative influences. A circle of salt can be placed around a bed for the same reason. (You can use it, for example, when you move into a new apartment or house to cleanse it.)

Water

Water is the last of the elements consecrated for use in the circle. It's associated with the west and relates to purification of the body. This should come as no surprise since for centuries we've been told to drink lots of water "to clean out the system." As one of the substances necessary to sustain life it's natural that water should be included as one of the four basic elements. The water is combined with the salt for the purification of the circle, thus allowing for the purification of both sides of life—physical and spiritual—at the same time.

Bell

The bell used in the circle is a simple, small glass or porcelain bell that is placed on the altar or, in some cases, placed at the East quarterpoint. Don't use a metal bell unless it happens to be the metal associated with the planet you're working with. (Some traditions do allow silver to be used at any time as it is associated with the goddess.)

The bell has basically one purpose, with some variations. It provides sound to obtain the attention of spirits. In loud, random ringing it acts to repel unwanted entities from your surroundings (much like oriental wind chimes are expected to do). If used carefully and deliberately, the bell becomes part of a ritual to summon a specific entity. For instance, it can be used in the east to summon the Lord of the Watchtower of Air. In ceremonial, if the planet you're working with is in an air sign, it would be appropriate for you to utilize a bell in the ritual, ringing it the number of times represented by the number of the planet.

The Robe

The robe is a somewhat ticklish matter. There are so many variations as to style and color that no rule can be offered as to what, if anything you should make. Many people never use a robe at all, preferring to wear whatever's handy. Others prefer wearing nothing at all. Some say the robe should have a hood; others say the head should always be bare. Some say the robe should be black; others say the robe should be white; others say the color of the robe depends on the level achieved by (or bestowed upon) the person (red, green, yellow, white, or whatever). Some say you have to make it yourself; others say there's nothing wrong with the robe being store-bought or sewn for you by someone else.

Do what you'd like if you're working alone or do what you're told if working with an established group. Working "skyclad" has the advantages of no physical restriction on the body and no fear of being ignited by a candle. Also, it puts you in more direct contact with the earth, making it more effective as a source of energy. On the other hand, skyclad is somewhat awkward if you're working outside in winter. Generally, a hoodless, white or black robe is a safe compromise, since both leave chakras in the head uncovered and retain most energy they encounter. If you want to use another color, consider the associations of that color first. You may want a single robe for everything, or you might want a different color robe for each potential application (red for Mars, orange for Mercury, purple for Jupiter, etc.) Either way is okay.

Whether you make it or buy it, the robe should at least be cleansed before using it and might also be consecrated. You can easily put a simple cleansing ritual together for yourself, centered around the idea of purification by the four elements. Consecration would be done in a similar manner, after the cleansing, backed with the intent that the robe will serve as a working tool that will attract and retain energy and power for you.

Generally speaking, a robe used for Craft workings should not be used for ceremonial, too. If you're going to be using both forms of magick, separately, have two different robes. Also, if you decide to have a robe for each planet and consecrate each to the appropriate planet, use it only when you call upon an entity associated with that planet. In other words, you can call on the sun if you're wearing a red (Mars) robe, but if the robe has been consecrated to Mars, wear something else (or else wear nothing at all).

Talismans

The manufacture and use of talismans is an entire school of magick unto itself that can get so detailed and picky that few have the patience for it anymore, even though it was one of the most widely practiced forms of magick. The aspect of talismanic magick we're concerned with here relates to the use of talismans in the evocation of spirits.

In Appendix E you'll find a sample ritual for the consecration of a planetary talisman. The principle involved here is that once a talisman has been consecrated or endorsed by the spirit for whom it was made, the magician has virtually unlimited control over that spirit. It isn't really unlimited, of course, but it does make future evocations a lot easier. The consecration I'm referring to is the placement of the mark of the entity on the talisman *by that entity* as a sign of acceptance and cooperation. In part, it represents an agreement between you that the talisman will serve as a link to the entity through which it can be called.

Talismans are usually made on the metal of the appropriate planet or, lacking that, drawn on parchment. If done on metal, use the kerfan to inscribe it with the signs, sigils, numbers, etc., of the planet and entity you want to summon. If done on parchment, draw the same things using india ink. (You can find the information in *The Golden Dawn*.[12]) Generally it's best to make them in the hour and day of the appropriate planet, too, in a circle with the candles and incense of the planet. In effect, set up for a full ritual based on the planet, make the talisman in the circle, then have it consecrated, all at the same time. It should all flow together neatly and effectively.

• • •

That's basically what goes into a circle as far as the material elements are concerned. You can use whatever you want as containers (like a chalice for the water), candlestick holders, dishes and bowls, but usually these are either silver, porcelain or glass (the metal of the goddess or else something neutral). Candles can be hand-dipped or store-bought. Incenses can be made of hand-picked herbs or courtesy of McCormick and your supermarket's vegetable section.

As time goes on you'll probably want to get more formal and do as much as possible for yourself. Your athame, chalice and candlestick holders, for instance, will be made of silver and inscribed with appropriate runes, symbols or whatever. You'll probably grow your own herbs to be harvested at a particular time and dried for incense, paying more attention to things like phases

---

[12]Israel Regardie, *The Golden Dawn* (St. Paul, MN: Llewellyn Publications, 1971).

of the moon and planetary relationships. It all comes in time, and it's frequently tied in with the level of success you achieve in your work—the more successful you are, the more likely you are to invest the additional time and money to get everything just right so you can maximize your power.

Consecration and Deconsecration

One last thing we need to cover on the subject of your working tools involves matters of consecration and deconsecration. In Appendix D you'll find a ritual for consecrating an athame. You always consecrate that first because it's used for everything else. Everything you use regularly in the circle should be consecrated. You can use the athame consecration ritual as a model for the rest.

When you consecrate a tool, you're charging it with your own energy and marking it as something special to be used only in rituals. While you can use any glass as a chalice for the water and you can use any candlestick holder you happen to have around for the candles, once you've decided to use an object for your rituals, use it only for your rituals.

The time may come when you want to use something new or different in place of what you've been using. When that happens, you need to do two things: consecrate the new tool and *deconsecrate* the old one. You need to break the connecting link between that object and yourself as well as to break the connection between that object and whatever planes, deities or entities you've been working with. Deconsecration is not a minor technicality, and you can't afford to forget or ignore it. If you've been using an object as a working tool and then decide you don't want to use it anymore, deconsecrate it.

CHAPTER NINE

The Ritual

W E'VE COVERED WHAT MATERIALS go into a magickal ritual. By now you should have a pretty good idea of how to prepare yourself physically and mentally. You should have your athame, wand, candles and everything else that goes on the altar ready and waiting. Presumably you've made the decision as to whether you want to utilize a ceremonial approach or one of the various pagan traditions, and you know whether you're going to be working alone. Finally, you should have decided on specifically what you intend to do and how you're going to picture it and describe it when the time comes. Now we're going to start putting it all together into a workable format.

While most people believe that every element of a ritual must be done in precisely the right way and in precisely the right order, this isn't exactly necessary. Certainly there are basic outlines which can (and should) be followed, but there's a lot of leeway for suiting your own tastes and inclinations. If you understand the basics of how a ritual is constructed you should be able to create your own, utilizing whatever elements from Wicca or ceremonial that suit you personally, even if it comes out as a combination of both Wicca and ceremonial.

Think of a ritual as like a house. First you select the type you prefer, but you still have only a framework. Many people will argue that everything in a ritual is laid out in advance and you must follow the guidelines exactly, like buying a house that's already furnished. Think for yourself. This book gives you that framework; you can customize the details in whatever way suits you for your own comfort. It is extremely important that you feel comfortable with everything you're doing; if you're not, it won't work for you. If rearranging the furniture (rewriting a ritual) isn't going to be enough for you, scrap it all and start over (with a different tradition). You have read repeatedly that different traditions do things in different ways. This should reassure you that experimenting is acceptable and that workable rituals can be constructed from scratch given a basic outline to follow. Following is that basic outline.

In broad terms, a magick ritual is composed of the following steps:

- Setting up the circle and altar

- Personal preparation

- Cleansing the area

- Consecrating the elements

- Casting the circle

- Summoning the protective elements

- Invocations/Evocations

- Banishing everything

- Closing the circle

We've already discussed the first steps—deciding what you want to do, what (who) you want to call upon to help you do it, and deciding when to do it. The next step is defining the area you are going to use for your circle and setting up the necessary tools on the altar. *Write an outline of what you're going to do.* This is especially important for those just starting out; you might find it helpful to write out the entire ritual word for word. This will help you organize your thoughts, clarify what you want to do, remember sequencing if you get lost somewhere in the course of the ritual, and will serve as a record of what you've done that can be reused later. Still, it's also a good idea for everyone to prepare at least an outline before doing any ritual.

Once that's done you need to settle down again into the proper frame of mind for the work. Relax, mentally rehearse the ritual and go over the desired end result one more time.

Begin the actual ritual by cleansing the area of all unwanted influences, then consecrate the elements and cast the circle itself. After the circle has been formed, you'll summon the Lords of the Watchtowers and any other appropriate protective elements and then the entity or entities you want to do the work for you. Finally, dismiss those whom you've asked to protect you, cleanse the area with a general banishing, and close the circle by extin-guishing the quarterpoint candles and mentally storing the circle itself in the ground.

Another important element of magickal work involves sound. Sound is a form of energy and possesses its own characteristics. People involved in magick have always believed that *how* you say something often can be as important as *what* you say. In many books containing rituals you'll find the idea of vibrating a name, command or whatever. By pronouncing a word carefully, distinctly and forcefully, you are creating an energy field of sorts and setting up a vibrational pattern that can affect the various entities with which you deal, making your ritual more effective. In calling upon a particular entity, if you use all the resonance your body can provide to your voice, the quality of the sound will make it easier to contact that entity. Merely saying the name as you would in everyday conversation would carry a lot less force.

This principle was particularly important in the Egyptian magick tradition which put heavy emphasis on words of power. It was believed that anything could be done if you used the proper words (sounds) and pronounced them properly. For instance, in *Egyptian Magic*, Budge offers this translation referring to Isis: ". . . she was strong of tongue, and uttered the words of power which she knew with correct pronunciation, and halted not in her speech, and was perfect both in giving the command and in saying the word."[13]

As for names themselves, an ancient belief was that knowing the true name of someone or something gave you power over that person or thing. That's why, for instance, Isis tricked Ra into revealing his true name by creating a serpent to poison him and then convincing him that only by knowing his name could she cure him. This is also the foundation of the practice of having a secret name revealed only to those who are trusted beyond question. Many pagan traditions also have secret names for their deities. Sometimes different names are used at different levels of personal advancement. Those individuals who have achieved a higher level are given a name to call upon that gives them more power and/or authority over the entity being called upon or worshipped. In the Hebrew tradition, even God had a secret name that was kept secret and was never to be said by anyone. You may remember reading or hearing stories about exorcisms in which the first order of business was to get the demon to reveal its name. The idea, of course, was that once you had the name you had more power over it.

Always remember names, pronounce them accurately, and put some force behind them when you speak (vibrate) them.

Set Up the Circle and Altar

First, physically define the circle as discussed, resolving the questions of size, shape, location and design. Put your quarterpoint candles in their proper places and if you're going to use other

---

[13]Sir E. A. Wallis Budge, *Egyptian Magic* (Secaucus, NJ: Citadel Press, 1978), p. 129.

symbols for the elements, put them out too. (Put something under the candles to minimize clean-up afterwards.)

Next, set up the altar. Put down the appropriate color altar cloth, then your candles, water, salt, incense and whatever you'll be burning it in, and your athame. These are the bare-bone essentials that you lay out roughly according to the diagram in the chapter on the circle and tools. If you're doing a ceremonial ritual you'll need to add the various paraphernalia associated with the planet with which you'll be working: candles, metal, planetary incense, plants/flowers, talisman, etc. For a pagan ritual add the god and goddess candles, maybe a statue, flowers, pentagram, and anything else you feel is appropriate to the work or the season. Check the earlier illustration for guidance on these altar arrangements.

Before starting, disconnect the phone. You don't need the distraction during the ritual and whoever it is can call back later. Anything else that could cause a disturbance or distraction should be addressed at this point. Whatever you need to do to assure privacy, such as closing the blinds or locking the doors, you should do now. Establish your sense of physical security so you can put it out of your mind. Check around and think ahead to anything that might distract you from your work once you get started. Whether it's a baby who may get hungry or a dripping faucet, take care of it in advance so that once you begin you can continue to the end without interruptions.

Finally, remember you are dealing with energy here and different forms of energy can act on each other in ways that can interfere with what you're trying to accomplish. Electrical energy can be a source of interference, so turn off any fans or air conditioners (unless it would make conditions absolutely intolerable), radios, television sets, and lights. You'll have a candle or two or three on your altar for light when you need it; some people like to light their god and goddess candles beforehand as focal points for their meditations. If it's electrical, turn it off, unless by turning it off you would create a distraction or worry.

Personal Preparation

Once everything is physically set up and ready to go for the ritual, you need to take time out to prepare yourself. The first step is to get into the proper frame of mind. This process should develop into a kind of ritual in itself that you can use any time you need it, whether or not you intend to follow it with a ritual. To start with, you need to relax. Find a comfortable sitting position and take a few deep breaths, inhaling slowly, holding it for a few moments, then exhaling slowly. Take your time; if you've started preparing early enough, you'll be ready before the proper hour to begin has arrived.

Relax. Picture all the tension and nervousness in your body draining away out your toes. Focus your attention on each part of your body in sequence—toes, calves, thighs, abdomen—right up to your scalp. Don't skip anything. Take your time, and when you're done, use your mind to double-check each part of your body for any lingering tension. If you find any, get rid of it. By all means talk to yourself in the process. Statements such as "All the tension is draining from my arms," just repeated in your head, will contribute to the relaxation process. As you say it, visualize the tension flowing out of you.

After the process of releasing the tension, you'll start to concentrate your attention on one thing at a time, whether it's the performance of the ritual or the end result you hope to achieve. By the time you're done you should feel very relaxed, your breathing will be deep, slow and regular, and your mind somewhat open and free-flowing, but ready to focus itself and to visualize anything you want. You're pretty much exactly where you want to be both physically and mentally and this is the state you want to work from, regardless of what that work is. In the context we're discussing at the moment, that happens to be the performance of a ritual, but that doesn't have to be the case. From this point you can do a lot, from reaching out with your mind to check on someone, to creating a familiar, to contacting entities on other planes for information. This relaxation process is essential to any type of work you want to do.

The next step is to take a ritual bath while maintaining that relaxed and open feeling. A nice, relaxing hot bath with some bath salts or herbs or flower petals appropriate to the planet you'll be working with is just the thing to help you stay physically relaxed and get yourself presentably clean in the process.

Just lie back, relax and think about what it is you're going to be doing. Since you've already (supposedly) achieved something of the state of mind you need for the ritual, this is an excellent chance to rehearse the ritual in your mind, step-by-step, from the initial banishing ritual and invocations of the protective entities, through the summonings to the final banishing. If you're going to be calling on something to help you, picture in your mind where you'll be standing in the circle, what you're going to say and do, and see your invoked deity entering you, or the entity coming up to the circle or entering the outside triangle (whatever's appropriate to your ritual), knowing that it will, indeed, come when summoned.

Then hold the image of the desired end result you're working for, keeping in mind the importance of seeing it as already accomplished, not something that will happen in the future. (If you picture it as happening in the future, it will always *be* in the *future*.) While this procedure for preparing yourself may seem like an unnecessary effort, remember: (1) everything that helps to put you in the proper state of mind or to keep you there contributes to your chances of success, and (2) all the thought and energy you put into the visualizations in this preparatory stage will have a positive influence on either performing the ritual itself or on the desired end result.

Finish up your bath, dry off and go on to your circle (dress is optional) while continuing to maintain your relaxed, meditative attitude. It's very important at this stage to quell any sense of fear, anxiety or doubt that might still linger. If you've rehearsed the entire ritual in your mind and you're certain of what you're going to be doing, you shouldn't have any anxiety about goofing up the ritual and appearing foolish. If your concentration is good, the circle will be good and strong and should serve to protect you against anything that might put in an appearance. All of that's another part of the reason for this mental preparation stage. After a while anxiety and doubt won't be a problem anymore. Finally, have faith. No one can guarantee that any particular ritual will work completely every time for everyone, but if you've followed the general principles given here, chances are that at worst you'll have started to set up the necessary energy patterns above that will increase the probability of getting what you want here below.

Now in practical terms there are problems involved with going through all of this if you're working with a group. Having a line of people waiting to take a bath isn't conducive to mental comfort or concentration. All this preparation is intended to relax the body and focus the mind. The high priest and high priestess, or magician, should go through this ritual preparation immediately prior to the working ritual in any event. If there are too many others to allow for a quick shower, let them go through the physical cleansing at home before they come and settle for that. (If they get dirty and sweaty on the way over, you can't do much about it, unless it's enough to be a distraction, in which case you'd *better* do something about it.)

If you're with a group, immediately before entering the area of your intended circle, take time to discuss exactly what you're going to be doing, why, and what each individual is expected to do in the course of the ritual. This review will usually help put everyone into the proper frame of mind. Then go through the relaxation exercise outlined earlier, perhaps with one of you actually verbalizing it step-by-step for the others.

Once you feel you're ready, get everyone in position, including yourself in front of your altar. By this time everyone should be in a fairly controlled state of mind, with attention focused on what's being done and nothing else. The ordeals you have to face at work tomorrow have no place in the circle (unless that's what the ritual is going to be addressing, of course). Put everything not relating to the work at hand out of your mind and keep it out of your mind until you're done.

Cleansing the Area

Pick up your athame, take a few deep breaths and once more focus your mind only on what you're about to do. If you're working with others, have them do the same. The first thing you want to do in the circle is to make sure you're starting from a neutral environment, without any little gnomes or demons or other kinds of disembodied curiosity seekers hanging around. You can do this with a general banishing ritual. Personally, I like using the Lesser Banishing Ritual of the Pentagram (LBR). While the LBR is, strictly speaking a ceremonial ritual, I like to use it to start everything, even a pagan-based ritual. It's easy to do (once you learn the language), it can be done anywhere, even outside of your traditional working area, it's generally effective for cleaning out any room, and it serves as a final trigger for concentration and general mood.

In a pagan ceremony you may want to begin with a simple invocation to set the mood for the gathering. As a mood-setting piece and/or introduction to the work to be done you may choose to compose your own opening invocation. If you do, keep it fairly short. It's intended to set the mood for what comes afterward and is not intended to be magickal in its own right. Here's a sample you can use:

> Let all here take heed of my words for this place shall be a place of worship—a temple to the goddess and the god. Let this circle be in a place that is not a place. Let this be a time that is not a time, on a day that is not a day, between the worlds and beyond.

Naturally, if you're not practicing one of the pagan traditions you'll need to make a number of changes in this, but it still makes for a good starting point, particularly if you're working with a group. This would precede the LBR.

The LBR is a good all-around banishing ritual which you can (and should) use to open and close everything you do, regardless of tradition. It can also stand alone as a straight-out banishing ritual independent of any other ritual. It serves two purposes at the same time: to clean the area in which you're going to be working of all entities and lingering energies that could interfere with your work and to seal your own aura, helping to protect you from being directly affected by anything that's attracted by your ritual.

Lesser Banishing Ritual of the Pentagram

Start with your athame or sword in your right hand, face to the east, and relax for a moment. Take a few deep breaths, get yourself into the proper frame of mind, and then begin.

The LBR starts and ends with the Cabalistic Cross. Holding the athame with both hands, put the hilt to the top of your head with the point straight up and say (vibrate):

A TEH

Keeping the point always upright, bring the athame straight down to the genital area and say:

MALKUTH

Next, bring the athame to the right shoulder with

VE-GEBURAH

(vay gah-BORE-a) and then the left shoulder with

VE-GEDULAH

(vay gah-DOO-la). Put your arms out to your sides, upper arms parallel to the ground, lower arms extended upwards.

LE-OLAHM

(lay o-LAM) Finally, cross your arms, fists to your shoulders.

AMEN.

Loosely translated, what you are saying is "For to thee (or Unto thee) the kingdom, and the power and the glory to the ages, amen." Sound more familiar in English? Probably, but keep it in the Hebrew for effect.

After you've completed the Cabalistic Cross, move on to the Lesser Banishing Ritual itself. Still facing east, draw the banishing pentagram of earth in the air in front of you. Visualize the pentagram as fiery blue light and then stab at the center, picturing the whole pentagram glowing brighter and stronger as you do so. As you make the stabbing motion, "vibrate" the name

YODHEVAUHE

The closest I can get to printing the pronunciation is "yud-HAY-va-hay."

Continue to hold the blade straight out in front of you and turn to face the south with the blade tip drawing an arc of light over the intended perimeter of the circle. When you reach the South, draw another pentagram in the air in front of you. (There are two options at this point. Some people continue to use the Earth Banishing pentagram at all four quarterpoints. Others prefer to use the banishing pentagram appropriate to that direction. The latter makes more sense to me, but the former is more common. You can make your own choice.) Again stab at the center, turning on the pentagram, and say

ELOHIM

(el-o-HEEM). Once more turn with the point out in front of you and picture the arc continuing to glow and expand from the center of the southern pentagram around to the west. Draw the banishing pentagram of earth or water, turn it on with the stab to the center, and say

EHEIEH

(ay-HEE-uh). Continue around to the north in the same manner, drawing the circle as you go and the pentagram at the quarter-point. The name you use in the North is

AGLA

(AH-glah). Now close the circle by extending it from the north pentagram around to the east, terminating in the center of the pentagram there. You are now surrounded by a circle of bright bluish-white light with flaming pentagrams at the four quarter-points. Stand there facing toward the east with your arms stretched out straight from your sides (being careful not to stab anybody in the circle with you) and finish with the following:

> Before me, Raphael; behind me, Gabriel; at my right hand, Michael; at my left hand, Auriel; about me flames the pentagram, and in the column stands the six-rayed star.

Having said that, cross your arms over your chest, close your eyes and once more visualize the entire circle around you blazing away and setting up a barrier that will keep everything away from you.

You may want to do one other thing at this point in addition to or in place of the LBR, which I'll describe without going into too many details or explanations. First, using your wand, draw a circle around you about waist high, turning yourself around to draw it. See the circle in your head as your trace it and imagine it as a real line of force that will stay there around you. Next, draw a second circle the same way, starting from straight over your head, down and to the left, on around to the right side and back up again. Finally, draw a third circle around you starting from the same point over your head, down around in front of you, up behind you and back to the top. You now have three intersecting circles traced in each of the three planes. These have a somewhat arcane symbolism, but it's sufficient that you recognize them as a form of protection.

Consecrating the Elements

The next step is to consecrate the elements used to cast the circle. I've provided two different versions here—one pagan and one ceremonial—and you can take your choice. Either can be done solo or with a group; if done solo, just leave on the altar what another person would be holding.

The purpose of these consecrations is to cleanse the elements themselves of any negative influences they might have so they can then form an uncontaminated circle. Keep this in mind and, as you prepare each element, imagine your energy flowing into the element and charging it.

Consecration of the Elements—Pagan

The high priestess holds her athame in her right hand and the high priest holds a chalice of water. They face each other and the high priestess puts the point of the athame into the chalice and states:

> I exorcise thee, O creature of Water, that all impurities and uncleanliness be cast out from thee. This I do in the names of [goddess] and [god].

The chalice of water then is set back on the altar and the high priestess takes up the bowl or dish of salt and, again facing the high priest, places the point of the athame in the salt and blesses it:

> Blessings upon thee, O creature of Salt. Let all malignity pass on and let all good enter in, and let us all be mindful that as water purifies the body, so does salt purify the soul. This I do in the names of [goddess] and [god].

She then uses the point of the athame to transfer three measures of salt into the chalice of water and stirs it three times in a clockwise direction.

Next is the consecration of the incense. The high priestess takes up the incense and blesses it as follows:

> Blessings upon thee O creature of Air. I charge thee let no phantom in thy presence stay. This I do in the names of [goddess] and [god].

A measure or two of the incense is then placed on the charcoal and the invoking pentagram of air is drawn horizontally in the smoke. After this, the salt water and incense are ready to be used for casting the circle.

Consecration of the Elements—Ceremonial

If you're using ceremonial magick, there is no high priestess or high priest (by definition), so you'll be doing almost everything yourself. The procedure is pretty much the same either way, putting your athame into the water, the salt, mixing the salt into the water and stirring. The procedure for the incense is also the same.

The consecrations (exorcisms) for the ceremonial ritual go like this:

> I exorcise thee, creature of Water, in the name of God, Almighty Father, and in the name of Raphael, Michael, Gabriel and Auriel, thy servants, Archangels of the Most High, that all illusions may depart from thee, all phantoms and ghosts, demons and devils, shapes and shells, and all wickedness and uncleanness may flee from thy presence, and that thou mayest serve as a helpful remedy for both mind and body. Amen.

> I exorcise thee, creature of Salt, by the living God, by the God of Gods, and the Lord of Lords, that all illusions may depart from thee, all phantoms, demons, devils, shapes and shells, and that thou mayest serve as a helpful remedy for both mind and body. Amen.

I exorcise thee, O creature of Air, by Him who hath made all things! Do thou expel from thee all phantoms, so that they may in no wise harm or trouble us in our work, by the invocation of the Most high Creator. Amen.

Casting the Circle

Once all the elements have been consecrated, you can proceed with casting the circle. Begin, as with everything else, at the east and moving around the circle in a clockwise direction. The general practice is to start with the athame or sword, presenting it (holding it up) to the east, and then tracing the outline of the perimeter of the circle with its tip (right over the circle you traced with the LBR), going around the whole thing three times while visualizing the circle itself growing stronger.

Next, throw some more incense on the charcoal and repeat the same procedure of presenting it to the east and tracing the circle three times. (If you're working with someone else it might be both helpful and wise to have that person ready to put more incense on the charcoal since some burn rather quickly.)

Finally, repeat the process using the salt and water mixture, sprinkling (not pouring) the water around the circle. As before, try to visualize the circle as you move around it and see it growing brighter and stronger each time around.

If you're using a pagan ritual, acknowledge the completion of the circle with something like this:

I charge this circle of power be a boundary between the worlds of mortal men and the Ancient Ones. May kindness and love be guarded and protected in the names of [goddess] and [god].

You now have your circle. Don't cross the line. Don't let anyone else cross the line. (Yes, there are exceptions. If there's an emergency you can use your athame to cut an exit in the circle to let someone out and then you can close it up again as soon as they're clear, but that's only in case of an *emergency*.) Usually, if the circle is broken for any reason, the smart thing to do is forget about trying to mend it and recast the whole thing from scratch.

Summoning the Protective Elements

Various protective elements can be called upon to help guard your circle. The LBR called upon the archangels of each quarter-point to come and lend a hand with this. Another group of guardians is referred to as the "Lords of the Watchtowers."

In preparing for the circle you placed a candle at each quarterpoint and maybe a bell at the East, candle at the South, water in the West and Earth to the North. These are symbolic of the elements associated with those points. First, the high priest-ess, escorted by the high priest, goes to the East point (always moving clockwise around the circle, starting from behind the altar) where they salute the quarterpoint. The salute is done by lightly kissing the athame and extending it out in front of you towards the quarterpoint at an upward angle. If there is anyone else present in the circle for all of this, they, too, will offer a salute to each quarterpoint at the same time as the high priestess and high priest, maintaining the position of the arm extended towards the quarterpoint while the high priest rings the bell softly and the high priestess recites (with feeling)

> Hear me, O ancient and mighty ones of the East, ele-ment of Air. I summon you to witness our rites and to guard and bless this circle.

Everyone concludes the salute by once again kissing the athame lightly, extending the arm straight out and up the same way as before, and then returning the arm to the side. The high priestess and high priest next move to the south where the high priest lights the extra candle, everyone salutes and the high priestess does the evocation:

> Hear me, O ancient and mighty ones of the South, element of Fire. I summon you to witness our rites and to guard and bless this circle.

Again, the salute is concluded and they circle to the west and the bowl of water that was placed there. The high priest will pour a small amount of the water from the bowl during this evocation.

> Hear me, O ancient and mighty ones of the West, element of Water. I summon you to witness our rites and to guard and bless this circle.

The salute to the west is finished. The last remaining quarter-point, of course, is that of North and earth. Once more all salute, and the high priest will spill a little of the soil (or salt) from the bowl.

> Hear me, O ancient and mighty ones of the North, element of Earth. I summon you to witness our rites and to guard and bless this circle.

Then the high priestess and high priest return to the altar.

Now, there are a lot of variations to this, depending on the tradition. Differences occur based on personal preferences and comfort. In some cases the angel associated with that point is called by name. Sometimes the specific name of the king or ruler of the element is used (check the table of elemental correspondences in Appendix C for names).

There are also variations on how the elements are presented to the quarterpoints. In some instances, the consecrated salt and water are put on a tray along with the bell and candle and carried by the high priest. At the East he will take the bell from the tray, ring it and, in some instances, leave it there. In the south he will light the candle from the tray and leave it. In the west, some of the consecrated water would be poured into a bowl placed there or it may be poured onto the ground. The same in the north with the salt.

The basic principle is to present the appropriate element at the appropriate quarterpoint and call for the presence and protection of an associated entity, whether that happens to be an angel, elemental king, or whatever you choose (as long as it is appropriate to that element). Try different approaches and then settle on the one that feels most comfortable and effective for you.

Next comes the business part of the ritual. This is where you call on the entity you want to help with your work or where you offer your petition to the goddess and god or build up your energy (individually or as a group) to be sent out to do your work.

Evocations—Ceremonial

For a ceremonial ritual you are going to use a lot of materials related to the appropriate planet. Let's say you want to do a ritual to help a business and decide to use Saturn for this purpose. First, you will want to do the ritual on a Saturday (the day of Saturn), probably in the evening at the hour of Saturn, calculated as outlined earlier. It would be preferable to do it during a waxing moon but before the full moon. If the planet happens to be in the sign of Capricorn, so much the better.

Next, you'll want to have three (the number of Saturn) black (the color of Saturn) candles on the altar as well as a piece of lead (the metal of Saturn). The incense will be the planetary oil or can be made up of one or more of the herbs associated with the planet and perhaps some flowers and/or live plants from the list. If you've previously prepared a talisman for Saturn, that would be placed on the altar, also. (For Saturn I'd use Cassiel, but you can make your own choice.)

When you come to the proper place in the ritual, bring everything appropriate to the planet together near you, light the three candles and put more incense on the fire. Get yourself into the proper frame of mind, then call the entity, such as Cassiel, whom you've chosen to work with. Ceremonial rituals have a strong tendency to become complicated and long- winded at this point. I've included some in Appendix E to serve as examples. These include how to create an elemental familiar out of the physical elements themselves, and instructions on the consecration of planetary talismans that can be used afterwards as part of the ritual to summon an entity associated with that planet. Steps 2, 3, 4, 6 and 7 are pretty universal for ceremonial rituals.

The conjuration itself (step 4) can be very long or very short, depending on your experience, what you're summoning and what your purpose is. It's possible that you will create a certain rapport with an entity to the extent that it will actually come *before* being specifically summoned, because through all your mental preparation up to this point the message got through that you were about to call. Even if that happens, still go through something of the standard procedure. It's usually better to overdo something than to underdo it, and never take anything for granted. The same holds true for steps 6 and 7, having to do with the final banishing.

How can you tell if an entity you've summoned has answered the call? One possibility is the development of a heavy stench driven by a gale-force wind that will shatter everything in the room until the walls buckle outward because of the tremendous size of the entity. Another possibility is that you'll stand in the middle of the circle listening to the traffic outside and wondering what you did wrong. Guess which is more likely.

Like a lot of other things here, this is something you'll just have to develop a feel for. In most cases there will not be any physical manifestation to let you know that an angel or demon or whatever has entered the room. There may be a slight flickering of the candles or a trace of an odor in the air, but don't count on it. This is where the development of your psychic abilities and your ability to focus and concentrate become critical. Depending on your own particular talents, you should be able to see, feel or hear whatever you've summoned. Descriptions of appearances vary greatly depending on whose work you're referencing and what entity you're summoning, but actual physical appearances are rare. What you're likely to get is an emanation of the energy of the entity being called rather than a manifestation. Since most things function better on the astral plane, if you can meet them at that level you'll be better off anyway.

If you see or sense a presence in the room that feels right, continue the ritual; if not, repeat it. Unless there's some verbal communication between you, you're probably not going to know what has appeared, but you might as well continue under the assumption that you're in the presence of what you called for. (Feeling a positive reaction to the incense, sigil, candles, and other planetary symbols, would be an encouraging sign.)

This is where it helps to work with someone else. While there's certainly something to be said for direct communication, you may need to keep your concentration centered on what you're actually doing without stopping for anything that would break your concentration. The benefit of having another individual(s) with you in the circle is that this person can open up psychically to determine when (if) the entity has actually answered the summons and what its response is to any question or statement put to it. This helps to maintain a safe mental distance between you and the entity.

When you're satisfied that the entity has come, tell it what you want it to do. Be specific; don't mince words, but don't behave like you're dealing with some kind of slave. Cooperation is much better than coercion, so phrase it as a formal request rather than a demand. Try to leave as little leeway for independent decision-making as possible. You need to find a balance between being general enough to allow some flexibility, which can accelerate things, versus being specific enough to minimize the risk of extensive negative repercussions while extending indefinitely the time it would take to meet all your conditions.

Once you have given the instructions, request acknowledgment and understanding of the instructions and a positive agreement to perform the deed requested. At this point things can start becoming a little hairy, depending on what you've called up and asked for. In most cases you should get an agreement fairly readily, but if you're not sure, go through the entire requesting procedure again. If you continue to face resistance, you can become a little more demanding and forceful, moving from request to demand in tone and phrasing.

While there is certainly a long written history of dire warnings that have been used against uncooperative demons, I suggest you forget about it. Usually more than one entity can help you with a given request. You may have to reword the request or rethink your approach, but if you think about it a while you can come up with an alternative. Gaining the cooperation of an alternative entity is preferable to trying to command one that may become angry and eventually try to stab you in the back. As with the energy you deal with in all things, magickal and otherwise, follow the path of least resistance and you'll be most productive.

In spite of all this discussion about evoking an entity, you should consider the possibility of invoking an *aspect* of an entity—something of its nature rather than its person—for matters of self-improvement or for help in an internalized fashion. Using the Mercury example, you can call on the aspect of Raphael or Tiriel relating to eloquence if you need to give a speech or the aspect of intelligence if you need to take an exam. Or if you are, by nature, shy and introverted, you could call on Zamael of Mars for courage, strength and those attributes associated with self-confidence and self-assertion, working to have those attributes permanently incorporated into your personality.

Working with planetary entities needn't be limited to matters of a physical nature or to non-physical items external to the operator; they can be internalized. Magick can be used to cause a change in the personality. That's not necessarily bad and is sometimes something that should be sought and taken advantage of. If you examine yourself objectively, you'll probably find characteristics you'd like to change or feel should be changed; calling upon the nature of a planet can help. You can *invoke* the strength of Mars or the mercy of Jupiter, the compassion of the Sun or the love of Venus.

Once you've received the acknowledgment and agreement you want—or given up trying—dismiss the entity you've called. Even if you don't think it ever came, assume it has and dismiss it. Here's an example of a "License to Depart":

> Because thou camest in peace and quietness in answer
> to my command I give thee and thine license to depart.
> Go in peace and quit this circle. Return to thy domain
> in the silence, but only come again should I again
> require thee and by thy name and seal to conjure thee.
> Go in peace.

When you've finished, check out the room to make sure it's gone. If you have any doubt at all, repeat the License to Depart until you're certain you're alone.

Invocations/Evocations—Pagan

In the pagan traditions, there are a variety of different types of rituals, not all of them intended to perform an act of magick. Some are primarily religious in nature while others are a combination of religion and magick, intended either to evoke the goddess or god or to invoke them into the high priestess or high priest prior to the magickal portion of the ritual. However, there's really no such thing as a purely religious ritual because at the minimum you're giving energy to the god(dess)-form that can be tapped later. Likewise, no Wiccan ritual is purely a working ritual since it entails acknowledgment and invocation of the deity(ies) of the tradition.

In Appendix D are the Invocation to Diana and a ritual called Drawing Down the Moon. On the face of it, neither of these would seem to have anything to do with magick or power, but they do. The Invocation to Diana (and any variations you create for yourself) can serve as a kind of mood-setter. All magick has its root in the mind, so anything you can use to create a more suitable frame of mind is useful. This is particularly important when you're leading a group because you really need to orchestrate the mood, the attitude, the feeling and activity of everyone in the circle in order to produce the harmony and unity of mind and purpose necessary to make the ritual work. That's part of what it means to be a leader and, specifically, high priest or priestess. Always remember that the way you act and sound in the circle will have a direct bearing on the attitude the others will have toward you, the circle and the work to be done, and that's going to have a profound effect on your chances for success.

The Invocation to Diana is pretty simple and can be used to open any ritual of suitable tradition once the casting of the circle has been completed. Naturally, if you're working in an Egyptian tradition you'd use something a little different, since the symbolism associated with Isis or Hathor or whomever you've chosen is different from the symbolism associated with Diana. The same holds for any other tradition. Familiarize yourself with the attributes and symbolism of the deities of the primary tradition in which you've chosen to work. If you do that properly you should be able to compose an appropriate invocation for opening your rituals and for most other purposes, too.

Drawing Down the Moon can also serve as a mood-setter, but it has another, more important purpose. The concept behind Drawing Down the Moon is to invoke the entity of the goddess into the high priestess. The high priestess serves in the circle as the representative of the goddess to begin with; this invocation is intended to accentuate the direct tie between Above and Below—the goddess and her priestess—allowing (in theory) for the physical possession of the latter by the former. The goddess is intended to take physical possession of the priestess. I say "in theory" because the actual possession rarely takes place.

People involved with ceremonial magick never advocate opening yourself to possession by *anything*. That's not a bad policy for everyone to follow, especially the novice. When you're doing Drawing Down the Moon, regardless of intent, you're offering yourself up to being possessed. Unless you're really good, you won't have any control over what may end up possessing you. You may intend for it to be your goddess, but that doesn't mean something else might not beat her out or enter with her at the same time and remain long after she's gone. Regardless of what you may have thought when you bought this book, *magick is not a game*. Physical and outright permanent mental possession is a real possibility that you have to guard against, and that's something I can't emphasize enough.

The Invocation of Diana and Drawing Down the Moon are introductory rituals, in that they're not intended to perform an act of magick. If the circle is limited to these two acts, you'll have a basically religious ritual and not a magickal one. That's okay, though, because becoming familiar with the ritual itself will make you more comfortable with performing future rituals, and the concentration and visualization involved in performing these two rites will put energy into the form of the goddess that can come back to you in the future when you need it, not totally unlike recharging a battery.

The business part of the pagan ritual will vary a great deal depending on who you're working with and what you want to do. In Appendix D you'll find a ritual for consecrating your athame, which is one you definitely should undertake before you try any others. Certain principles regarding the generation and concentration of energy come into play for all rituals. While the circle is being cast, everyone is concentrating on and contributing to the energy being used to create the circle, later they help to summon the Lords of the Watchtowers. At each step of the way all members of the circle should be concentrating on what's being done and contributing their individual energies to the person performing the ritual, whether high priest or high priestess. Traditionally the female leads the ritual. The male—especially if he's more experienced—can take the lead, in which case the energy and attention would be directed more at him than his partner.

If you're working alone, settle down once more, relax and start thinking again about the end result you're seeking. If you need to, go through the whole relaxation exercise again. *See* all the energy within the circle circulating around the boundaries, building up more and more speed and brilliance. Consciously draw more energy into yourself from above and picture that energy contributing to the massive flow encircling you.

If you're working with a single compatible individual, at this point you'll face each other—standing or sitting, preferably palm-to-palm—and work at building up the energy flow between you. Just imagine a river of white light flowing down into your body, filling it, and then the current flowing out your right arm to your partner and back into your left. See this energy field growing around you and then expanding to fill the whole circle.

If you're working with a group, the above will still apply to what the one or two people leading the ritual will be doing, but there are two things the others can involve themselves with at this point to help. One is to join hands and concentrate on building up the energy field around the high priestess and/or high priest, picturing the energy flowing down through and around them or, alternatively, concentrating on picturing the desired end result. The second thing would be to start walking clockwise around the circle, with a rhythmic step, hands joined, chanting something related to the nature of the work being done while again concentrating on either building up the energy or picturing the end result. (While something like "OM" might seem appropriately mystical to some and attractive as a chant, it is better to use something more relevant to the work at hand that will aid your concentration on the subject.)

The high priest works at helping to concentrate all the available energy into the high priestess, while she concentrates on maintaining the image of what you're working for and directing all the energy she's receiving into that image. When she's satisfied that the image of the desired end result is firmly in mind and the energy has been built up sufficiently to bring it into reality, then everything can be released. If there are other people in the circle, give them a signal of some kind, at which point they direct all of their combined energies at the high priestess and picture all of the energy that has been confined by the circle rushing to the center and then up and out through her. The high priestess continues to maintain the image of what's desired and pictures all the energy within her (including what everyone else is channelling into her) flowing up and out of the circle carrying that image with it.

There are differing opinions as to whether the entire group or just the high priestess should be concentrating on the end result at any given time. One group suggests that with everyone picturing the common goal the energy will be that much more directed. Others believe that it's too unusual for any two individuals to picture the same thing in exactly the same way and that by having two or more people all trying to put the same energy into different images the work becomes self-defeating, so only the high priestess should be involved with the image while the others focus unrefined energy to her.

I tend to go along with the latter view, with the additional argument that if the members of the general group concentrate their attention on producing the energy and guiding it to the high priestess, they'll be focused on one subject (the energy) rather than two (the energy and the goal) which makes them more effective individually and also helps guard against any possible negative feelings that someone might hold against the work itself, which could certainly interfere with the success of the ritual.

That's the basic outline of the pagan magick ritual. If you combine this with the theory discussed in earlier chapters, you should be able to write your own effective ritual—both the words and the actions. It really isn't that hard to do. You may even feel more at ease and confident in a ritual you've prepared yourself rather than in one you've tried to memorize word-for-word from a book. As I've said repeatedly, there's nothing wrong with experimenting once you've got the basics down pat. Try different things in different ways to find out what you're most comfortable with and what's most productive. Just remember not to skip any steps in the ritual. You can change the language and you've even got some flexibility in the form, but don't skip something important (like the banishings).

Another, simpler ritual that you can do either alone or with any number of other people is the Ritual of Incense Petitioning, which harkens back to the time of sacrifices being made to the gods. Most pagan religions today are very pro-nature and pro-life, abhorring the sacrifice of animals or people; instead they use various forms of symbolic sacrifice such as this one. Sacrifices—blood or symbolic—may be related to the idea that everything has a price. While we now interpret this in more personal terms, in the past many sacrifices were offered not for the energy they contributed to rituals but rather in settlement for something being requested. Sacrifice to the Rain God is one example that comes readily to mind.

Ritual of Incense Petitioning

The high priestess begins by placing a little incense on the charcoal and saying:

> Hear us, oh Ancient Ones. Though you ask nothing in
> the way of sacrifice, accept these offerings and hear our
> petitions. Blessed Be.

She then holds her hand over the rising smoke from the incense, meditates a few moments upon what she wants, then removes her hand, urging the smoke upward, symbolically letting the smoke carry her wish to the skies. The charcoal and incense are then passed to the high priest, who may repeat the process for a wish of his own. He, in turn, may then pass the charcoal and incense around the circle so everyone else may make their own wishes.

While it's rather simple in nature, the Ritual of Incense Petitioning carries all the important elements of the standard magick ritual: evocation, meditation, concentration, and release. It has the advantage of being so simple and easy that it can be made a part of just about any type of circle you hold. Let's say you have a small group together to discuss something you've been reading or experimenting with and you decide to do it within a circle. Before you break up you can do the Ritual of Incense Petitioning, giving everyone a chance to utilize some of the energy you've built up within the circle during your conversation.

Banish Everything

This is the part of a ritual that more people get wrong or skip entirely than any other, sometimes with very uncomfortable results. Banishing isn't all that hard. The LBR that started this ritual, for instance, is quite easy once you become accustomed to it. The problem is that many people tend to think that it's a good thing to have a lot of entities around so it will be easier to summon and command them. Some people like the idea of having them around and actually try using them for an ego trip: "Something feels funny in here." "Oh, that's just an elemental I conjured up last night."

And some have the mistaken idea that if these entities are still around they'll provide on-going protection. Not so.

Let's consider some of the hazards of not banishing the entities you've called and attracted. They can make themselves felt in a number of ways. They can drain you of energy or they can leave you feeling jittery all the time, unable to relax. They can keep you awake at night or cause continuous nightmares, either of which will leave you feeling exhausted the next day. They can effect personality changes, making you depressed, paranoid, touchy, erratic, obnoxious, aggravating, aggressive, and generally unsociable and unhappy in any number of ways. They can influence every aspect of your life, personal and professional. Technically, by failing to banish all entities you could end up broke, unemployed, homeless, sick, alone and even institutionalized, since some entities, in time, can effect a complete physical and mental possession.

If that's not enough to encourage you to clean up after yourself, then consider this: anyone who's around you or staying in the same place the ritual was done can be subjected to the same effects I've just mentioned. If you don't care about yourself, think about what you might be doing to others. If you don't, there may be hell to pay later.

This is particularly true if you're doing ceremonial rituals. These tend to attract more entities of a different order than most pagan/Wiccan rituals, so it is that much more important to do the banishings. Generally, the License to Depart and the LBR should be enough to clear out any spirits you've called or attracted. You can't be too careful, nor can you overdo it. If you have *any* doubt in your mind as to whether or not everything has been cleared out, do it again.

First, you need to dismiss the Lords of the Watchtowers. To do this, the high priest and high priestess circle clockwise around the altar to start at the east quarterpoint; once there they extinguish (snuff, not blow out) the quarterpoint candle. Everyone salutes the quarterpoint as was done in the original evocation, and while maintaining the salute, the high priestess will dismiss the Lord of the Watchtower (or the king or whomever she had called for protection) with something along these lines:

License to Depart

Hear me, O ancient and mighty ones of the East, element of Air. We thank you for answering our call to protect and bless this circle. Return now to your airy domain, and as you depart we bid you Hail and Farewell! Go in peace.

All in the circle repeat "Go in peace" and then kiss their athames and salute once more. The high priestess and high priest then move around to the south while the others turn in place.

At the south quarterpoint, the high priest will extinguish the candle, all salute and the high priestess gives the license to depart:

> Hear me, O ancient and mighty ones of the South, element of Fire. We thank you for answering our call to protect and bless this circle. Return now to your fiery domain, and as you depart we bid you Hail and Farewell! Go in peace.

All in the circle repeat "Go in peace," kiss their athames and salute once more. The high priestess and high priest then circle to the west where the procedure is repeated.

> Hear me, O ancient and mighty ones of the West, element of Water. We thank you for answering our call to protect and bless this circle. Return now to your watery domain, and as you depart we bid you Hail and Farewell! Go in peace.

All in the circle repeat "Go in peace" and salute as before. The high priestess and high priest proceed to the north.

> Hear me, O ancient and mighty ones of the North, element of Earth. We thank you for answering our call to protect and bless this circle. Return now to your domain, and as you depart we bid you Hail and Farewell! Go in peace.

All in the circle repeat "Go in peace" and kiss their athames for the last time. The high priestess and high priest salute to the east once more as they circle around back to their place at the altar.

At this point I suggest that you use the LBR once more.

One more time: while I did say that the need to banish everything was particularly true of ceremonial rituals, don't take that to mean you don't have to worry about it if you're performing a Wiccan ritual. You do. *Always* worry about it. Though it's likely you'll only be dealing with elementals and the like as far as random visitors are concerned in a Wiccan ritual, you can't take that for granted. That's another reason I like to use the Lesser Banishing Ritual for both ceremonial and pagan circles.

Closing the Circle

The high priestess has two final things to do, starting with the storing of the circle. For this she returns to the East quarterpoint and uses the tip of her athame to trace the circle *counter*-clockwise. As she does this she should picture the light of the circle sinking into the ground and staying there rather than being extinguished. By doing this, the circle will be stored in place. Each time you repeat the ritual creating the circle you'll actually be building on top of this foundation, so each circle should be stronger than the previous one, all else being equal. Each time you create a circle you set up an energy pattern that will remain for a long time. By stressing the desire for it to remain rather than disappear, you will cause it to stay longer and stronger than it would have otherwise.

At this point the work is done, the banishing (hopefully) completed and the circle can be broken. You can, if you want, offer a formal conclusion to the ritual for the benefit of any others with whom you may have been working. A simple one many groups use goes like this:

> We thank the Ancient Ones for attending. May all power be yours. The circle is broken; the rites are ended. Blessed be.

The Orgy

The orgy doesn't really fit in as a part of a ritual, but since many people associate witchcraft and orgies, I thought this would be a good place to address that subject.

Remember that the old pagan traditions were and are basically nature-oriented religions. This means that (1) sex was/is considered a natural act and (2) sex was used as a means to encourage crop growth and animal reproduction using the principles of sympathetic magick. Having sex was okay, though it's doubtful that orgies, as we understand and use the term, were ever a part of the magick rituals.

Aside from the naturalness of sex, there was a more immediate, practical reason for a gathering to end in sexual intercourse. In the course of a well-done ritual, participants try to put themselves in direct contact with other planes. A lot of energy is generated and released through a ritual. Sex is a very quick, effective and pleasant way to ground your energies and return fully to this world. The exchange of energies that takes place between two individuals with physical forms on this plane, when not accompanied by the intent to reach another plane, will serve to rebalance and revitalize both. Sexual intercourse was used as a tool to break off contact with and sensitivity to the astral/psychic side and get back down to earth. (Please note, I am not advocating this as a portion of any ritual; it is offered by way of explanation of a common misconception.)

Follow-Up

That's it. Now, maybe your ritual has worked and maybe it hasn't. Generally, it's better to believe it did work because you don't want to send out any negative vibrations that might counteract your effort. There will be times when you will feel certain that you've been wasting your time. Maybe your concentration was wandering too much or you repeatedly messed up the ritual; maybe there were too many distractions; maybe it just felt wrong. These things do happen. Don't let it get you down. Maybe there's a reason you weren't supposed to make it work and you just weren't informed by the Powers That Be what that reason is, in which case you need to find out why. Maybe the timing was wrong. There could be a lot of legitimate reasons. You don't have to take it personally.

If you're reasonably certain the ritual isn't going to work, try it again some other time. Repetition can't hurt unless you get carried away with it. Reinforcement is good; creating a rut is not. If you do try again and the ritual still doesn't seem to come out right, consider the possibility that you're doing something wrong with the ritual itself. Make sure that you've got the right materials on hand, such as the proper incense, metal, etc. If you're using a ritual you've composed yourself, look it over and think about changing the wording somehow. Also consider the possibility that you're trying to do something that shouldn't be done for some reason and just let it go.

On the other hand, if you've been working with others, don't overlook the possibility that the interference is closer at hand than you thought. Disbelief *will* have an effect on a ritual. The stronger the individual's energy and the stronger the disbelief, the more likely it is that the entire ritual will be sabotaged by that person.

In any event, don't let yourself get discouraged. Keep trying, keeping in mind that practice makes perfect. Experiment with different ritual formats, different planets, different entities, even different participants. Maybe try a different tradition if you're using a pagan system. A lot of things can be approached in different ways. It's important to find the one combination with which you're going to be most comfortable.

Finally, the last thing you need to do is keep records of what you've done. Whether you're writing out the full ritual or just doing an outline, keep those records in a book and date them. Take particular care to note exactly what the ritual was meant to do, plus anything that occurred during the ritual other than what you planned. Were there an unusually large number of distractions? Did someone smell something or hear something the others didn't? Were any errors made in the ritual itself?

The reason for this is that someday you may need to find out why something happened (or didn't happen). I've often heard stories from people who had strange things happen to them that they couldn't explain. Going back to their records, they've usually found a ritual they did and forgot about, or something included as part of a ritual, or something that happened during a ritual, that could explain the strange event. Sometimes it only takes seeing on paper exactly how you worded a request to explain a later mystery.

Things happen all the time to those who have started using their psychic and magickal powers—socially, professionally, mentally—and sometimes you'll be able to learn a lot from looking back on the records of rituals you've done. Practically speaking, if something significant goes wrong, your record will be a big help to review exactly what it was you did at the time as well as your observations of the moment on anything that occurred during the ritual.

A good written record also will be a way to trace your own development, your successes and failures, and how you've changed over the years in which you'll be practicing magick. That's a pretty good reason in itself to write down everything that you do or that happens to you. Like a photo album, it may become priceless to you in the future.

CHAPTER TEN

Other Methods of Magick

WE'VE TALKED ALMOST SOLELY about forms of magick that utilize a ritual performed in a circle. Now we're going to take a brief look at other methods of performing magick. Three in particular are sex magick, candle magick and what I call mental magick.

Sex Magick

Sex is probably one of the oldest methods for generating energy for magickal purposes and it's still used a great deal today, especially by so-called primitive religions. When done for magickal purposes, intercourse (or masturbation) is a long, slow process intended to build up as much tension as possible, delaying orgasm until the last possible moment while concentrating on the work intended.

Sexual stimulation and excitement can produce a lot of physical tension that can be translated into a lot of energy. The more time spent on foreplay, the more energy you should have to send out; but you've got to keep your mind on why you're doing it. The idea is to produce energy that can be directed at a particular piece of magical work. If you get too wrapped up in the sensation of sex, you'll lose that intent and concentration and nothing will be accomplished beyond the physical enjoyment of the moment. This brings us back to concentration.

If you've ever indulged in fantasizing during intercourse, you know you can see a picture in your mind of someone (or something) totally different from the picture you get through your eyes. This picture doesn't get in the way of physical sensation, either. Simply put, then, in sex magick you build up the sexual tension as long and high as you can, keeping in mind your purpose. At the moment of orgasm you release all that tension/ power into the mental picture you've created that reflects the end result you want. The energy is projected up to the astral plane with that picture, hopefully bringing about a change on that level that will then be reflected back on this plane, just as with other forms of magick. (After the energy is sent out, you can feel free to collapse to your body's content.)

Sex magick, when there's a partner involved, can be particularly effective not only because of the nature and quantity of energy generated, but also because there *is* someone else involved. There are two of you involved (orgies don't count here) and the energy increases geometrically; as was mentioned earlier, two people working together generate more energy than two people working separately.

Another reason for doing this with another person is because of the polarities involved. When positive and negative polarities are present, there is a flow of energy between them that makes it easier for the energy to build up. Male feeds female, female feeds male (or male-to-male, female-to-female, as the case may be), the energy flows back and forth in ever-increasing magnitude until both release it to the same image. The more freely your energy can flow within you (during intercourse you both would constitute one person), the more energy you'll have and the more effective you can be. Having both positive and negative polarities present helps the energy flow more freely.

On the other hand, anything you can do with someone else, you can try doing alone. While fantasizing during masturbation probably won't give you the same level of energy that can be raised during intercourse, energy is still generated and it can be guided into a visualization of your desired end results like any other energy under any other circumstances. Probably the most common application of solo sex magick is in combination with a Venus ritual to do work involving love or sex. This is not the only thing you can use it for, but it's the most common use.

Candle Magick

Candle magick is considered by many to be the easiest form of magick. Basically, it involves lighting a candle of the appropriate color for the desired end result, concentrating and visualizing the result, then letting the burning of the candle send the idea out to the astral plane to work. *Everybody* has tried to perform candle magick, at least once a year. Did you ever make a wish and blow out the candles on a birthday cake? Or light a candle in church?

This is a form of the As Above, So Below principle of magick, based on the premise that the burning of a candle of the color associated with the desired end result will have an effect on the appropriate environment. Candles of different colors are associated with different effects, and this choice is frequently tied in with the colors of the human aura. Red, for instance, is associated with passion, whether that passion is anger or lust. These qualities can appear in the aura the same way. ("Seeing red.") The same holds for the association of pink with love. Green, the color of nature, can be used for balance (as in the balance of nature) or for money (though this is mainly an American association), while lime green acts for matters involving jealousy ("green with envy"). It is all a matter of affecting the symbol to affect the thing being symbolized.

In Appendix C you'll find a listing of some candle colors and their associations. In truth, a number of books are dedicated solely to the practice of candle magick, and most books written by witches also contain similar lists; frequently there are major differences in all these lists. One reason for this is that different people often associate different colors with different aspects of life. Consider money as an example. Americans may use a green candle because all their paper money is green, but people in other countries might use any of a number of colors because their currencies are printed in different colors for each denomination.

The procedure for performing candle magick is rather simple, which is why it's so common. You start with a candle of the appropriate color, preferably one that is solid in color rather than white on the inside and colored on the outside. You can inscribe the candle with anything that seems suitable to your work, such as a person's name, monetary symbols, the signs for Mars or Venus (male or female) or anything else. Some people anoint the candle by rubbing an oil onto it. (The appropriate oil can be determined by looking through the planetary correspondences in Appendix B.) Around the candle you can put any other objects that relate in your mind to the object of your desired end results. If it involves a person, for instance, you might have a photograph, a lock of hair, some object the person gave you, etc. Light the candle and sit or kneel comfortably in front of it while you concentrate your attention on the candle and what you want to accomplish.

Keep the picture of your desired end result sharp in your mind as you watch the candle. Try to project that picture into the candle and flame, imagining the smoke carrying the message of your desire to the heavens. If you can, accompany all this with an appropriate chant and/or prayer stating what you want to accomplish. Burning an appropriate incense at the same time also helps. When you're done, leave the candle burning until it burns itself out. If this would constitute a safety hazard though, go ahead and put it out, but unlike a birthday candle, *don't* blow it out— snuff it. Use a candlesnuffer or your dry finger (don't mix the elements of fire and water) to put it out. One theory for this is that by blowing it out you would be dissipating the energy while in snuffing it out you're still leaving it concentrated.

Finally, I reiterate: don't just sit back and expect the candle to do everything for you. If there's something you want, do something positive to help and give it the opportunity to happen. The gods help those who help themselves.

Mental Magick

Basically, the only difference between mental magick and everything else we've talked about is the lack of ritual, deities, paraphernalia, candles, everything but your own mind and will. All magick is essentially mental in nature and just about everything else is intended to condition the mind to make it easier. (Other kinds of work such as "Path Workings" do take place on other planes and utilize the assistance of entities on those planes, but that's far more advanced than is intended for this book.)

The principle of doing mental magick is that you get comfortable, relax, visualize the desired end result, concentrate on it and project all your energy into the image being visualized, keeping in mind that you want it in the present tense and not in the future. As I said, all that's lacking are the accoutrements of ritual. In terms of preparation, mental magick is much easier than a ritual, but in application it's more difficult because the mental preparation for the work is accomplished through concentration and will power and nothing else.

A simple example of mental magick is making the wind blow. It involves nothing more than opening the mind to the feeling of the air and a breeze—in a manner of speaking, mentally becoming a part of the air, just as we talked about mentally projecting into animals—and then imagining putting the air into motion. It sounds simpler than it is, but it's really not all that difficult once you get the hang of it.

Some people have a knack for working with their minds alone; other people need the conditioning and self-hypnosis aspects provided through a ritual. I advocate using both. For instance, you might perform a ritual for something, then reinforce it by projecting additional energy into the visualization whenever you've got some free time to sit down, relax and work on it. You can also work mentally at a desired end result while waiting for the right time to perform a ritual.

As with everything else, the keys are desire and practice. If you keep working on visualizing things and projecting all your internal energy (as well as any external energy you can draw into yourself in the process) into that visualization, the time should come when you can perform magick any time and any place you need to. This is the ultimate form of magick and the one toward which everyone should be working.

CHAPTER ELEVEN

Knowledge

IN THE FIRST CHAPTER I talked about power and knowledge being paths of growth and development. We've talked a lot about power and looked at some of the knowledge needed to make it work, but everything we've covered so far should be considered as a starting point; it's far from being the complete story. I want to close this discussion of magick and power with a look at where all of this information has come from through the years and some thoughts as to how to obtain answers to any questions you may have now or in the future. I'm not referring to what books to read, but to the source of the information in those books. How were systems of magick developed to begin with?

Many times here you've been told to experiment with different traditions, different approaches, different rituals and wordings, to develop a system that will work best for you. No doubt one approach that's been used for centuries is trial and error plus observation, the scientific method. Given the belief that something was possible, people kept trying different methods to make it work. When a particular approach produced the results they were looking for they wrote it down or handed it down by word-of-mouth through the years.

Much of our knowledge of herbs probably came about this way. Diseases may not have had the same names or symptoms centuries ago that they have now, but through the years many cures were discovered by testing the effects of different plants and parts of plants until something was found that worked.

We can assume that some of the old information was gathered through experimenting with sympathetic magick, as well as through experimentation in general. What about the rest of the information, such as specific rituals, what should be in them and what names to use? As with magick itself, ultimately the answers had to come by looking inside. Through the use of psychic sensitivity, meditation, trances, etc., people asked questions in their heads and received answers from someone or someplace not of our physical world. Fortunately, what worked then can still work now, even though our materialistic world makes this approach somewhat more difficult than it once may have been.

Who or what do we need to contact in order to find the answers to our questions, and to understand some of the answers we've already received?

Memory

Whether you call it ancestral memory, racial memory, collective unconscious, or whatever, a pool of memory is available for people to tap into for answers. Some suggest this memory is in our genes, others say it's free-floating in the astral plane or it's a part of god. I don't know. Take your pick. It doesn't matter, really, as long as it's an available source of accurate information (which it is).

It's been hypothesized for hundreds of years that we carry within us the memories of everyone who has gone before us in history. Perhaps this type of racial memory is the root of what we call instinct. Unconsciously, we may tap into the history of our race to find answers to questions of immediate survival, for instance. This may also contribute to intuition and inspiration, particularly relating to questions of survival.

Another type of memory is personal, which takes us back to earlier references to reincarnation, in which you may or may not believe. The odds are good that you've have some contact with pagans, witches and/or magicians over the period of your existence, whether or not you have been one yourself, and the memories of those times can be drawn upon today. You can tap your personal memory for information. Chances are you've done this for many things in your life already, even if you're not aware of it. Becoming aware of the possibility will make it easier.

Learning to access these memories can not only supply you with a lot of answers about rituals and such, but also provide you with a lot of insight about yourself and other people. That is the beginning of knowledge and wisdom.

Akashic Records

I think of all the above as memory since the information being sought is somehow within you. Outside of you, however, are the Akashic Records that contain the same information, but also hold much more. Some say they contain *all* knowledge—past, present and future—as well as knowledge pertaining to other planets, other planes and other dimensions. The Akashic Records may be the same as, or an extension of, the collective unconscious or race memory and seem different only because of the amount of material credited with being available there.

The Akashic Records have been described as a giant library where you can obtain information on anything and everything. All you have to do is ask. You still need to know how to get there, and I'll get to that eventually.

Angels and Spirits

Entities that live on higher planes and have never incarnated in this world have more experience or have access to more information than most of us mortals. They're also a lot older and have better memories than we do.

If you look through the listings of the planetary correspondences and what kind of rituals each planet can be used for,
you'll notice a number of information-related entries: "answers
regarding the future" (Mercury), "communicating and speaking
with spirits" and "to acquire learning" (Saturn), "divination"
(Sun). This is a key source of information on anything and
everything. It's been used for centuries under the names "direct
revelation" and "divine revelation." It was probably through a
single, initial contact with a being of another plane that much
of today's knowledge of magick became available to us. Once
you've contacted an entity of a certain order, you should be able
to find out how to contact any other entity of that same order,
and probably more besides.

That doesn't necessarily mean they'll all answer you, by any
means, because your own nature, intent and level of development
will have a bearing on it. As with any attempts at dealing with
other entities, you can't assume they will cooperate simply because you asked them. Depending on the nature and level of
the entity you've conjured, some will be more cooperative than
others, some will always resist, but most will evaluate your request
on its merits and respond accordingly. Asking about a past life so
you can understand an aspect of yourself better is one thing;
asking about how to build a neutron ray gun is something else
entirely. I really wouldn't count on getting that kind of information if I were you.

Guides

Guides are spirits of varying types dedicated to helping a particular
individual or individuals. An entity can be dedicated to one
person or many, depending on its nature, the needs of the people
involved and what the entity itself is working to accomplish.
They can be a form of elemental, or possibly someone who has
had a physical existence in our world, or something else entirely.

Their origin isn't really that important because you can reasonably safely assume that your guide is capable of helping you in the areas where (cosmically speaking) you most need help.

Generally, guides are easy to contact and can be very helpful, but the range of information with which they can supply you is limited. They'll give you advice on matters that involve you personally, especially as they relate to your own development, and provide general guidance. Often your guide is the source of moments of inspiration and insight when you need it most.

Channelling

This is a controversial area and you will find a wide range of opinions on whether you should use this as a potential source of information. Channelling takes many forms, including the use of a pendulum, a ouija board or trance mediumship. In every case and form, however, the heart of channelling involves allowing a disembodied entity to have access to and control of your physical body, often (but not always) at the expense of your own consciousness.

You've been warned already about the risks of possession, and some degree of possession is essential for any type of channelling. The problem is that once you leave yourself open to serving as a channel for something, you're open as a channel for anything at all. From demon to angel to ghost to extra-terrestrial, you're welcoming one and all. While you're thinking about that, consider this: just because something doesn't have a physical body on our plane, doesn't mean it's omniscient, incorruptible or incapable of dishonesty. Some entities, including ghosts (disembodied human spirits), lie quite easily and convincingly, yet many people have a tendency to take as gospel anything said by beings from the other side.

That's not to say that this isn't a potentially useful way of obtaining information. A comparatively large number of advanced beings are now openly interacting with our world to advance its development. No doubt many more can and will come to help as more people develop the potential to operate as channels and become open to them. Maybe you'll be one of them.

A few recommendations if you are interested in this area: Don't jump into channelling until you've had some significant success either as a witch, magician or psychic. That experience will help you to handle the process of channelling and to judge the material received. Don't go into channelling alone. Have someone else with you, preferably someone you trust who has some knowledge and experience in the field. In view of the potential risks, this is an obvious safety precaution.

Keep a written or taped record of what occurs. If you do receive some information it's important that you get it right and memory can be a tricky thing, especially if you weren't conscious while the information was being delivered. A record is also important because most people want to believe what they're told by creatures from beyond the grave, and this can cause memory to become selective. By keeping a record of some form you can go back and double-check the accuracy at a later date. Never take for granted that anything must be true simply because it came from beyond. Test the information to establish the credibility of the source before accepting anything.

Making Contact

How *do* you make contact with any of these potential sources of information? Especially outside of a circle? Developing your psychic abilities is indispensable and crucial. Remember everything that's been said on the subject of possession. With that in mind, don't try anything aimed at making contact with any entity other than maybe your own guides unless you're with someone who can lend a hand if difficulties arise.

Another excellent reason to have someone else around is that verbal suggestion can be used to help you relax, to induce a trance and to help direct your mind to the specific source of information you're trying to reach. You may feel a surge of power and a sense of expanding your field of perception beyond yourself, and yet feel a loss of volition at the same time. Having someone there to help verbally guide your efforts can turn this potential negative (the loss of volition) into something positive by putting you in touch with your target through suggestion.

Re-read the material on relaxation and concentration in Chapter Nine under the heading "Personal Preparation." (No ritual bath is needed.) You're not going to contact anything if you're physically or mentally wound up. Just relax and perhaps let the person you're with use a countdown (counting slowly from ten to one) once or twice to help. Both the relaxation techniques and countdown can be used repeatedly until you're satisfied you're ready to continue.

The next step is to "simply" reach out (or in, as the case may be) with your mind towards whatever it is you want to contact and ask your question. You can use what I like to call the narrow band or broad band approach—visualizing a linking line between your mind and the specific entity you want to contact, or imagining the question radiating out of your head in all directions at once. This is an instance when you *don't* want to concentrate and focus your attention on your goal. Instead, you need to keep your mind as free and open as possible so the answers to your questions can flow in. You may get a picture of the answer or you may hear the answer or you may just suddenly *know* the answer, but if you don't open your mind to receive it, you won't get it.

If you're hoping to contact the Akashic Records, you can visualize a gigantic library and mentally scan through the building until your consciousness finds the answer. If you're trying to reach your guide(s), simply call on it and put the question. Contacting a guide is often the trigger for an involuntary channelling experience. In opening up for the information while deliberately invoking a spirit to supply it, other entities may come through.

If something else does come through, you may or may not retain consciousness. I know some people who simply step aside in their minds and let the channelled entity have the use of the body while still retaining ultimate authority and conscious control over it. Others are just out of it completely, with not the slightest idea of what occurred when the session's over. That doesn't make the information any more valid, mind you. Validity doesn't depend on how much you're aware of what's happening. The information needs to be tested to determine its validity; never take for granted that it's accurate. After a while you'll probably develop an intuitive feel for the accuracy of any information you obtain, but until you're sure of your source, question and doubt everybody and everything.

You *can* get information this way. In theory the entire universe is open to you if you can ask in the right way. Think of it as being covered by the general promise "Ask and it shall be given unto you." No one can promise that you'll get an answer every time. You can safely assume that there are certain questions to which no one will ever be given the answer. Nevertheless, you're encouraged to try often with whatever questions you have related to the information presented here. It may be a while before you can do it well— just recognizing the form of the information itself takes some getting used to—but keep at it.

An excellent starting question whenever you contact something is: "What are you and where are you?" If you want to learn what level or plane of existence an entity is on, ask it. Then open your mind for an answer and test the feel of it in your mind for accuracy. If you're not fully satisfied with the answer you get, ask again or ask for more detailed information. Keep probing until you feel like you've got a complete, truthful answer, even if it's not the answer you would have expected.

• • •

That's it, friends: you've got the basics. Try it, experiment with it, keep practicing, and when in doubt, ask for answers. You've got plenty of directions to choose from and eventually one of them will suit you to a tee. If you haven't become discouraged over all the choices you have to make and all the preparation you have to go through, then keep reading. You can start with some of the books on the list in the Bibliography. You can always request catalogs from the publishers listing other books they offer on the subject.

Do not expect immediate results from any of this. You may get some, but don't count on it. You will need to work with it a while to become comfortable with casting a circle and/or working with other people. Getting yourself into physical and mental shape also takes time. Keep at it and eventually you'll have enough power within you and available to you from other sources to change every aspect of your life virtually on command. Like any other talent, it takes time to develop but the results can be well worth the effort.

Invoking and Banishing Pentagrams

Earth

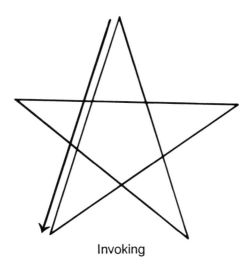

Invoking

Banishing

Air

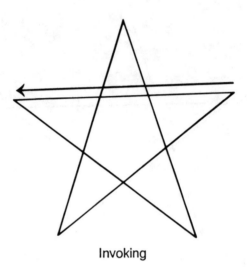

Invoking

Banishing

Fire

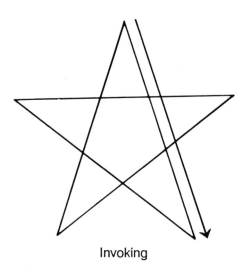

Invoking

Banishing

Water

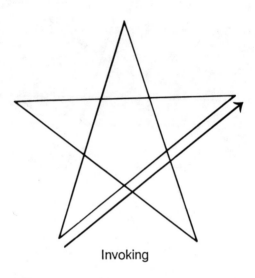

Invoking

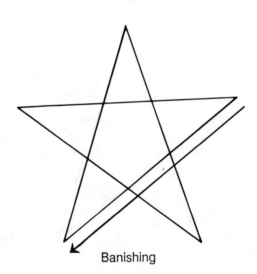

Banishing

Planetary Correspondences

Hours of the Planets
(Beginning at Dawn)

	Mon.	Tues.	Wed.	Thurs.	Fri.	Sat.	Sun.
1	Moon	Mars	Mercury	Jupiter	Venus	Saturn	Sun
2	Saturn	Sun	Moon	Mars	Mercury	Jupiter	Venus
3	Jupiter	Venus	Saturn	Sun	Moon	Mars	Mercury
4	Mars	Mercury	Jupiter	Venus	Saturn	Sun	Moon
5	Sun	Moon	Mars	Mercury	Jupiter	Venus	Saturn
6	Venus	Saturn	Sun	Moon	Mars	Mercury	Jupiter
7	Mercury	Jupiter	Venus	Saturn	Sun	Moon	Mars
8	Moon	Mars	Mercury	Jupiter	Venus	Saturn	Sun
9	Saturn	Sun	Moon	Mars	Mercury	Jupiter	Venus
10	Jupiter	Venus	Saturn	Sun	Moon	Mars	Mercury
11	Mars	Mercury	Jupiter	Venus	Saturn	Sun	Moon
12	Sun	Moon	Mars	Mercury	Jupiter	Venus	Saturn
1	Venus	Saturn	Sun	Moon	Mars	Mercury	Jupiter
2	Mercury	Jupiter	Venus	Saturn	Sun	Moon	Mars
3	Moon	Mars	Mercury	Jupiter	Venus	Saturn	Sun
4	Saturn	Sun	Moon	Mars	Mercury	Jupiter	Venus
5	Jupiter	Venus	Saturn	Sun	Moon	Mars	Mercury
6	Mars	Mercury	Jupiter	Venus	Saturn	Sun	Moon
7	Sun	Moon	Mars	Mercury	Jupiter	Venus	Saturn
8	Venus	Saturn	Sun	Moon	Mars	Mercury	Jupiter
9	Mercury	Jupiter	Venus	Saturn	Sun	Moon	Mars
10	Moon	Mars	Mercury	Jupiter	Venus	Saturn	Sun
11	Saturn	Sun	Moon	Mars	Mercury	Jupiter	Venus
12	Jupiter	Venus	Saturn	Sun	Moon	Mars	Mercury

Mercury

DAY:	Wednesday
NUMBER:	1
COLOR:	Orange
METAL:	Mercury
ZODIAC:	Gemini, Virgo
ANGEL:	Raphael
ARCHANGEL:	Michael
SPIRIT:	Taphthartharath
INTELLIGENCE:	Tiriel
HERBS:	Orange; dill; caroway; cinnamon; sandalwood; citron; lavender; fennel; hazel; licorice; mushroom; myrtle; valerian
IN THE HOUR:	Experiments relating to games, raillery, jests, sports
ON THE DAY:	To operate for eloquence and intelligence; promptitude in business; science; divination; wonders; apparitions; answers regarding the future; thefts; writings; deceit; merchandise; converse with spirits (especially when moon is in an air sign)
NOTES:	Mercury is very fast; hence, speed and communication are highlighted. One side of the planet is always hidden so it governs thefts and deceit.

Moon

DAY:	Monday
NUMBER:	2
COLOR:	Silver or White
METAL:	Silver
ZODIAC:	Cancer
ANGEL:	Gabriel
ARCHANGEL:	Gabriel
SPIRIT:	Chashmodai
INTELLIGENCE:	Malcah
HERBS:	Cedar; poppy; iris; lily; sassafras; lettuce; nutmeg; wintergreen; cucumber; turnip; watercress; willow
IN THE HOUR:	Recovery of stolen property; nocturnal visions; summon spirits to attend you in sleep; preparing for anything relating to water
ON THE DAY:	Embassies; envoys; voyages; navigation; messages; reconciliation; love; acquisition of merchandise by water
NOTES:	The moon governs the night and influences the oceans (water), which is what gives it influence over love, sleep, night visions and travelling.

Saturn

DAY:	Saturday
NUMBER:	3
COLOR:	Black
METAL:	Lead
ZODIAC:	Capricorn
ANGEL:	Cassiel
ARCHANGEL:	Tzaphqiel
SPIRIT:	Zazel
INTELLIGENCE:	Agiel
HERBS:	Juniper; yew; hemlock; hemp; henbane; holly; barley; beets; comfrey; cypress; elm; nightshade; poplar; safflower
IN THE HOUR:	Communicating and speaking with spirits; hatred; enmity; quarrels; discord
ON THE DAY:	To summon from Hades souls of those who died a natural death; good or bad fortune to buildings; to have spirits attend you in your sleep; to cause good or ill success to business, possessions, goods, seeds, fruits and similar things; to acquire learning; to bring destruction and death; to sow hatred and discord.

Jupiter

DAY:	Thursday
NUMBER:	4
COLOR:	Purple
METAL:	Tin
ZODIAC:	Sagittarius
ANGEL:	Sachiel
ARCHANGEL:	Tsadiqel (Zadkiel)
SPIRIT:	Hismael
INTELLIGENCE:	Yophiel
HERBS:	Maple; oak; asparagus; chestnut; dandelion; clove; hyssop; myrrh; sage; briar rose; fig tree; fir tree; jasmine; lime
IN THE HOUR:	Love; kindness; invisibility; all extraordinary, uncommon and unknown operations
ON THE DAY:	Obtaining honors, acquiring riches; contracting friendships; preserving health; "arriving at all that thou canst desire"
NOTES:	Jupiter is the largest of planets and is thus associated with abundance.

Mars

DAY: Tuesday
NUMBER: 5
COLOR: Red
METAL: Iron
ZODIAC: Aries
ANGEL: Zamael
ARCHANGEL: Khamael
SPIRIT: Bartzabel
INTELLIGENCE: Graphiel
HERBS: Cypress; dogwood; pine; nettle; garlic; onion; parsley; radish; tobacco; basil; ginger; broom; hawthorn; hops; mustard; pepper; tarragon
IN THE HOUR: Communicating and speak with spirits; summoning souls from Hades (especially those slain in battle); hatred; enmity; quarrels; discord
ON THE DAY: War; military honor; to acquire courage; to overthrow enemies; to cause ruin; slaughter; cruelty and discord; to wound or kill
NOTES: Mars is the god of war, so anything having to do with death and destruction should come under this planet.

Sun

DAY:	Sunday
NUMBER:	6
COLOR:	Gold or Yellow
METAL:	Gold
ZODIAC:	Leo
ANGEL:	Michael
ARCHANGEL:	Raphael
SPIRIT:	Sorath
INTELLIGENCE:	Nakhiel
HERBS:	Marigold; sunflower; frankincense; angelica; ash tree; bay; camomile; eyebright; mistletoe; peony; rice; saffron; walnut
IN THE HOUR:	Love; kindness; invisibility; all extraordinary, uncommon and unknown operations
ON THE DAY:	Temporal wealth; hope; gain; fortune; divination; to gain the favor of those in power; to dissolve hostile feelings; to make friends
NOTES:	The sun is bright and life-giving which yields to association with hope, love, etc., while gold relates to gain and wealth.

Venus

DAY:	Friday
NUMBER:	7
COLOR:	Green
METAL:	Copper
ZODIAC:	Taurus, Libra
ANGEL:	Anael
ARCHANGEL:	Haniel
SPIRIT:	Kedemel
INTELLIGENCE:	Hagiel
HERBS:	Strawberry; raspberry; apricot; daisy; violet; spearmint; thyme; bean; blackberry; catnip, cherry; goldenrod; geranium; mint; peach; pear; plum; rose; vervain
IN THE HOUR:	Love; kindness; invisibility; lots; poisons; preparing powders provocative of madness; all extraordinary, uncommon and unknown operations
ON THE DAY:	Forming friendships; kindness; love; for joyous and pleasant undertakings; travel
NOTES:	Anything sweet, tasty or pretty can be associated with Venus.

Candle Colors, and Correspondences to the Elements and Zodiac

Candle Colors

Black	Any ritual for extra power; communication with the dead; gaining spiritual understanding; to cause loss (of someone's power or loss of something); to cause discord or confusion.
Brown	Neutrality; hesitation; uncertainty; non-specific (can replace white; also can be used for gray, but is more subtle).
Blue (Dark)	Dispelling of evil forces; subduing; impulsiveness; depression; changeability.
Blue (Light)	Friendship; peace; harmony; joy; understanding; tranquility; patience; health.
Gray	To neutralize another's vibrations; to cause a stalemate; cancellation.
Green (Forest)	Money; business; financial gain; fertility; luck; Nature.
Green (Lime)	Sickness; cowardice; anger; jealousy; discord (99% baneful).
Gold	Represents the God; spiritual power; attraction; charm; confidence; persuasion.
Orange	Attraction; stimulation; concentration; encouragement; dreams; adaptability; peace of mind (a mental color).
Pink	Success; honor; morality; lesser degrees of love and sexual attraction.
Purple	Commanding; compelling; ambition; business progress; to cause tension.
Red	Love; sex; strength; health and vigor.
Silver	Represents the Goddess.
White	All-purpose; purity; truth; sincerity; peace; serenity.
Yellow	Same as gold; also for devotion; dispelling of evil.

The Elements and Their Correspondences

	EARTH	AIR	FIRE	WATER
Direction	North	East	South	West
Elemental	Gnomes	Sylphs	Salamanders	Undines
Archangel	Auriel	Raphael	Michael	Gabriel
Angel	Phorlath	Chassan	Aral	Taliahad
Ruler	Kerub	Ariel	Seraph	Tharsis
King	Ghob	Paralda	Djin	Nichsa
Tarot Suit	Pentacle	Wand	Sword	Cup
Ruling Sign	Taurus	Aquarius	Leo	Scorpio
Sex	Male	Female	Male or Sexless	Female
Qualities	Source of power	Creative Force	Justice, Intellect	Similar to Air
	Ancient	Thin	Tricky	(but weightier)
	Old	Young	Sinister	
	Slow	Quick	Fast	
		Ethereal		

Zodiac Colors

Aquarius	Violet
Pisces	Crimson
Aries	Scarlet
Taurus	Red or Orange
Gemini	Orange
Cancer	Amber
Leo	Greenish-yellow
Virgo	Yellowish-green
Libra	Emerald green
Scorpio	Greenish-blue
Sagittarius	Blue
Capricorn	Indigo

Pagan/Wiccan Rituals

Consecration of the Athame

Different traditions have different thoughts on how to consecrate an athame. Some take the position that a consecration can be performed only by a High Priest or High Priestess; others believe anyone can do it. For some, consecration includes the burying of the athame (or substitute any object) in the ground from full moon to full moon; others believe it doesn't matter. The term consecration suggests the dedication of the athame to a deity or religious principle, but this can be a self-limiting factor because any work you may want to do that is contrary to the nature of whatever the athame is consecrated to would be nullified automatically.

The purpose of the consecration is the dedication of the athame to performing magickal works by (1) setting it apart from ordinary objects so that it is used only within a circle, and (2) charging it with your energy so it has a power of its own that you can use for casting the circle and consecrating other ritual objects. On that basis, consecration in your own mind is more important than any kind of symbolic dedication to any deity.

The consecration involves the same principles as all the other magick: concentration, visualization, and will. Start by casting a circle. Once that's done, grasp the athame (or whatever object you're consecrating) in your stronger hand and concentrate all your willpower into it. Try to visualize all the energy around you flowing into your body, down your arm and into the athame, charging it, backed with the idea that it will become a magickal object to do work for you and that the power will continue to grow automatically from day to day. As you picture all this energy flowing into the athame, see it begin to glow and radiate this power from the blade.

While all of this can be done in silence, it wouldn't hurt to say aloud what you're doing: "I'm bringing the universal energy into my body and letting it flow into my athame, charging it with its power." Verbalize your desire that it become a magickal tool, that it hold the power being put into it and that it continue to absorb additional universal energy from its surroundings on a daily basis.

When you're done with the circle, put the athame away in a safe place. If it has a sheath, use it; if not, black silk makes for a nice cover. Remember never again to use it for anything not involved with working in a circle. The same holds true for any object that you choose to consecrate—athame, chalice, candles or whatever.

Invocation to Diana

The Invocation to Diana referred to in the chapter on performing rituals is a nice opening invocation for setting the mood for the rest of the ritual.

> Lovely Goddess of the bow! Lovely Goddess of the arrows! Of all hounds and of all hunting. Thou who wakest in starry heaven when the sun is sunk in slumber. Thou with moon upon thy forehead, who the chase by night preferrest unto hunting in the daylight with thy nymphs unto the music of the horn. Thyself the hunt-

ress and most powerful, I pray thee think, although but
for an instant, upon us who pray unto thee.

This is useful in its present form only for a tradition acknowl-
edging the goddess Diana; however, by studying the construction
and wording you should be able to modify it for whatever tradition
and goddess you care to use. Substitute the proper name and
images, keep the same close and you've got it.

Drawing Down the Moon

This invocation is used early in a circle, both to help set the
general mood and to invoke the presence of the goddess to assist
the group.

Even if no actual possession takes place after using this
invocation, if everything is falling into place properly a link will
be created between the two planes that make access to the energy
there much easier, and that's what you really want to accomplish.
Also, it will help accent the mood for the later work by providing
for the focusing of attention on a specific goal (the presence of
the goddess) and the use of energy to summon energy. The
repeated use of ritual procedures will put the participants further
into the proper frame of mind for the working ritual to come. It's
perfectly acceptable, if not preferable, for the high priestess to
concentrate on reaching out with her mind to the higher plane
rather than opening herself up to possession.

Leave the matter of opening yourself to possession until later
on when you're more experienced, more knowledgeable, and
have a good idea of how to handle it if something goes wrong.
On the other hand, this link can also be used as an information
source. Whether or not performing Drawing Down the Moon
leads to a link or a possession, the access to the other planes
implicit in the ritual should make it possible for answers to be
received to any questions put to the high priestess.

Drawing Down the Moon can be used as a transition between the opening aspects of the circle and the business side. The ritual has two parts: the invocation of the goddess herself, then the assumption of the goddess personality by the high priestess. The invocation is usually performed by the high priest, simply because having the male/female energy circuit is helpful and it's assumed that the person acting as high priest (the representative of the god) is the strongest and/or most knowledgeable person in the group. Drawing Down the Moon can be done by a lone female invoking the goddess (or the link) into herself (though not recommended because of the risk of possession and the accompanying lack of control), but it's not recommended for a male working by himself, though it's possible if his inclinations and polarity are suitable. *Please* recite it with some feeling and don't just mouth the words!

> I invoke Thee and call upon Thee, mother of us all, bringer of fruitfulness by seed and by root. I invoke Thee by stem and by bud. I invoke Thee by life and by love and call upon Thee to descend into the body of this, Thy Priestess and servant. Hear with her ears, speak with her tongue, touch with her hands, kiss with her lips, that thy servants may be fulfilled.

The high priest uses his energy and concentration to "Draw Down the Moon," meaning to draw the energy and personality of the goddess into the high priestess. While he recites the invocation, he should be seeing the goddess (or the link with the goddess) entering physically into the high priestess while she should be leaving herself open and receptive to the energy force.

The second part of the ritual is the charge, whereby the goddess, in the form of the high priestess, introduces herself to the gathering and gives her instructions. (Note the rhyming pattern used this time.)

> All ye assembled at my shrine,
> Mother Darksome and Divine;

Mine the Scourge and mine the Kiss
Here I charge you with this sign.

All ye assembled in my sight
Bow before my spirit bright.
Aphrodite, Arionhod,
Lover of the Horned God,
Mighty Queen of Witchery and night,
Morgan, Etoine, Nisene,
Diana, Brigid, Melusine:
So am I named of old by men,
Artemis and Cerridwen,
Hell's Dark Mistress, Heaven's Queen.

Ye who would ask of me a rune,
Or who would ask of me a boon,
Meet me in some secret glade
To dance my round in greenwood shade
By the light of the Full Moon.

In a place, wild and lone,
Dance about mine altar stone.
Work my holy mystery;
Ye who are feign to sorcery,
I bring ye secrets yet unknown.

No more shall ye know slavery,
Who give true worship unto me.
Ye who tread my round on Sabbat night,
Come ye naked to the rite
In token that ye be truly free.

I teach ye the mystery of rebirth;
Work ye my mysteries in mirth.
Heart joined to heart and lip to lip,
Five are the points of fellowship
That bring ye ecstasy on earth,
For I am the circle of rebirth.

I ask no sacrifice, but do bow.
No other law but Love I know;
By naught but Love may I be known.
All things living are mine own:
From me they come, to me they go.

That's the way it's been written and it certainly would be preferable to memorize it as is, but that's not essential. Do the best you
can and do it with feeling. Remember that you're speaking as the
goddess and behave accordingly. The important points are to
create the immediate link with the higher powers/energies, bring
that power down into the person acting as the high priestess,
then through the proper use of voice and body language, let
everyone else present know that the power is there, it's available,
and it's going to be used.

Some Ceremonial Rituals

Conjuration and Summoning of an Elemental

The following ceremonial ritual is used to create an elemental spirit for a particular purpose. The conjurations of the various elements, based on a combination of Eliphas Levi, Franz Bardon and the Golden Dawn, provide a good general idea of how such evocations are structured and can serve as a model for writing other rituals if you can't find one for the particular application you have in mind. Aside from its a practical application, study how it's put together so you'll have a feel for how to perform other rituals in the future.

    The elemental being created here is a real, living entity that you will assemble from each of the four elements conjured. (Being your own living creation, it's similar to a familiar, except the elemental is more restricted in purpose and has a well-defined life expectancy, whereas the familiar is more general and can be maintained for an extended period of time.) You give it a specific purpose—to cause something to happen, to influence someone, to investigate someone or something, whatever—and define the time of its existence. This means that the elemental spirit you create must be given a time to disintegrate and not permitted an indefinite life expectancy.

Keep in mind what was said earlier about responsibility. With this ritual your responsibilities are two-fold: you're responsible for what you direct the elemental to do and you're responsible for the elemental itself. Know precisely what you want your creation to do, keep it to one single task and define that task explicitly. Make sure nothing extra is included, and set the time for its dissolution-ment. As your creation, the elemental is an extension of yourself and anything it does is your personal responsibility. If you give it too much leeway and it does things you didn't intend for it to do, that's your problem in every sense of the word.

The ritual should take place in a properly consecrated circle in view of the four elements. Read the whole thing first so you understand it and get a good feeling for the various prayers and images. A "kylichor" should be drawn, which is where the ele-mental will be conjured, and placed upon the altar. (The kylichor is a regular octagon within a circle, drawn with red ink on white or yellow.) If you can't do that, a pentagram will do. A smaller kylichor can be made for you to carry. A seal or sigil that you'll use to summon the elemental should also be designed and drawn in the center of the kylichor. You will have to choose a name for the elemental in advance, as well as a specific time for its death.

Begin by casting the circle in the usual way, beginning with the LBR, but use all the invoking pentagrams in their proper quadrants. Follow this with a preliminary invocation and follow it with the following exorcisms:

Air

The Spirit of God moved upon the waters and breathed into the face of man the breath of life. Be, Michael, my leader, and Sabtabiel, my servant, in and by the Light. May my breath become a word, and I will rule the spirits of this creature of air; I will curb the steeds of the Sun by the will of my heart, by the thought of my mind, and by the apple of the right Eye. Therefore, I do exorcise thee, creature of air, by Pentagrammaton, and in the name Tetragrammaton, wherein are firm will and true faith. Amen. Sela. Fiat. So be it.

Prayer of the Sylphs

Trace the invoking pentagram of air.

Spirit of Light, spirit of wisdom, whose breath gives and takes away the form of all things. Thou before whom the life of every being is a shadow which transforms and a vapor which passes away. Thou who ascendest upon the clouds and dost fly upon the wings of the wind. Thou who breatheth forth and the limitless immensities are peopled. Thou who drawest in and all which came forth from thee unto thee returneth: endless movement in the eternal stability, be thou blessed forever! We praise thee, we bless thee in the fleeting empire of created light, of shadows, reflections and images; and we aspire without ceasing towards thine immutable and imperishable splendor. May the ray of thine intelligence and the warmth of thy love descend on us: that which is volatile shall be fixed, the shadow shall become body, the spirit of the air shall receive a soul, and dream be thought. We shall be swept away no more before the tempest, but shall bridle the winged steeds of the morning and guide the course of the evening winds, that we may flee into thy presence. O spirit of spirits, O eternal soul of souls, O imperishable breath of life, O creative sigh, O mouth which dost breathe forth and withdraw the life of all beings in the ebb and flow of thine eternal speech, which is the divine ocean of movement and of truth! Amen!

Exorcism of Salt

Breathe onto a bowl of salt.

May wisdom abide in this salt, and may it preserve our minds and bodies from all corruption, by Hochmael and in the virtue of Ruach-Hochmael! May the phantoms of Hyle depart herefrom; that it may become a heavenly salt, salt of the earth and earth of salt; that it may feed the threshing ox, and strengthen our hope with the horns of the flying bull! Amen.

Exorcism of the Ash

Breathe over the ashes of either burnt incense or of burnt palms.

May this ash return unto the fount of living waters. May it become a fertile earth. May it bring forth the Tree of Life, by the three names which are Netsach, Hod and Yesod, in the beginning and in the end, by alpha and omega, which are in the spirit of Azoth! Amen.

Exorcism of the Three Elements

Mix the salt, ash and water.

In the salt of eternal wisdom, in the water of regeneration, and in the ash whence the new earth springeth, be all things accomplished by Elohim, Gabriel, Raphael and Uriel, through the ages and aeons! Amen.

Exorcism of the Water

Hold both hands over the bowl of water.

Let there be a firmament in the midst of the waters and let it divide the waters from the waters; the things which are above are like unto the things which are below, and things below are like unto things above, for the performance of the wonders of one thing. The sun is its father, the moon its mother, the wind hath carried it in the belly thereof. It ascendeth from earth to heaven and again it descendeth from heaven to earth. I exorcise thee, creature of water, that thou mayest become unto men a mirror of the living God in His works, a fount of life and ablution of sins. Amen.

Prayer of the Undines

Dread King of the Sea, Who hast the keys of the flood-gates of heaven and dost confine the waters of the underworld in the caverns of the earth; King of the deluge and the floods of the springtime; Thou who dost unseal the sources of rivers and fountains; Thou who dost ordain moisture, which is like the blood of the earth, to become the sap of plants: Thee we adore and thee we invoke! Speak unto us, thine inconstant and unstable creatures, in the great tumults of the sea, and we shall tremble before thee. Speak unto us also in the murmur of limpid waters, and we shall yearn for thy love! O immensity into which flow all rivers of life, to be continually reborn in thee! O ocean of infinite perfections! Height which reflects thee in the depth; depth which exhales thee to the height, lead us unto true life by intelligence and love. Lead us to immortality by sacrifice, that we may be found worthy one day to offer thee water, blood and tears, for the remission of sins. Amen.

Exorcism of the Fire

Sprinkle the salt already prepared, some of which you have saved for this purpose, as well as incense, camphor and sulphur in small quantities onto a flame, and breathe thereon the three names of the genii of fire:

Michael, king of the sun and lightning, Samael, king of volcanos, and Anael, prince of the Astral Light.

Prayer of the Salamanders

Immortal, eternal, ineffable and uncreated Father of all things, who art borne upon the ever-rolling chariot of worlds which revolve unceasingly; Lord of ethereal immensities, where the throne of thy power is exalted, from which height thy terrible eyes discern all things and thy holy and beautiful ears unto all things hearken, hear thou thy children, who thou didst love before the ages began. For thy golden, thy grand, thine eternal majesty shines above the world and the heaven of the stars. Thou art exalted over them, O glittering fire! There dost thou shine; there dost thou commune with thyself in thine own splendor, and inexhaustible streams of light pour from thine essence for the nourishment of thine infinite spirit, which itself doth nourish all things and forms that inexhaustible treasure of substance ever ready for the generation which adapts it and appropriates the forms thou hast impressed on it from the beginning. From this spirit the three most holy kings, who surround thy throne and constitute thy court, derive also their origin, O universal father! O sole and only father of blessed mortals and immortals! In particular, thou hast created powers which are marvelously like unto thine eternal thought and thine adorable essence; thou hast established them higher than the angels, who proclaim thy will to the world. Finally, thou hast created us third in rank within our elementary empire. There our unceasing exercise is to praise thee and adore thy good pleasure. There we burn continually in our aspiration to possess thee. O father! O mother, most tender of all mothers! O admirable archetype of maternity and of pure love! O son, flower of sons! O form of all forms, soul, spirit, harmony and number of all things! Amen.

After this, the earth (the area you're working in) is asperged by sprinkling the water prepared above, by censing—called fumigation—with the incense and by bending low to the ground and breathing deeply on it, saying the following:

Prayer of the Gnomes

King invisible who, taking the earth as support didst furrow the abysses to fill them with thine omnipotence; thou whose name doth shake the vaults of the world; thou who causest the seven metals to flow through the veins of the rock, monarch of the seven lights, rewarder of the subterranean toilers, lead us into the desirable air and to the realm of splendor. We watch and we work unremittingly. We seek and hope, by the twelve stones of the Holy City, by the hidden talismans, by the pole of loadstone which passes through the center of the world! Saviour, saviour, saviour, have pity on those who suffer. Expand our hearts; detach and elevate our minds; enlarge our entire being! O stability and motion! O day clothed with night! O darkness veiled by splendor! O master who never keepest back the wages of thy laborers! O silver whiteness! O golden splendor! O crown of living and melodious diamonds! Thou who wearest the heaven on thy finger like a sapphire ring. Thou who concealest under earth, in the Stone Kingdom, the marvellous seed of stars, live, reign, be the eternal dispenser of the wealth whereof thou hast made us the wardens! Amen.

Conjuration of the Elemental Being

I do summon and conjure thee, elemental spirit _____ (name), being composed out of the four holy elements and bearing the seal of life upon thy forehead, that thou mayest aid and assist this present company in its undertakings. I charge thee to _____ (specify here what you want the elemental to do). Thou shalt perform this charge quickly, doing naught which has not been given unto you. Thou spirit _____, heed well thy name and remember thy charge, for thou hast a single purpose and a single goal. Neither shall ye harm this present company or any member thereof, but shall answer to it all the days of your life. Know that your life will end on the _____ day of _____ in the year _____ in the hour of _____, at which time your various elements will return to their respective sources. Arise! Move! Appear! Go to do thy solemn task!

Having conjured the elemental, the diagram of the conjuration is here rolled up and bound, to be opened again at any further summoning of the creature. The circle is now closed with the following exorcism to banish anything that might have attended the performance of the ritual and the creation of the living creature.

The Conjuration of the Seven

Cast incense seven times upon the brazier, saying:

In the name of Michael, may Jehovah command thee and drive thee hence Chavayoth! In the name of Gabriel, may Adonai command thee and drive thee hence Belial! In the name of Raphael, begone before Elohim, Sachabiel! By Samael Zebaoth, and in the name of Elohim Gibor, get thee hence Adramalech! By the divine and human name of Shaddai, and by the sign of the pentagram which I hold in my right hand, in the name of the angel Anael, by the power of Adam and of Heva, who are Yotchavah, begone Lilith! Let us rest in peace, Nahemah! By the holy Elohim and by the names of the genii Cassiel, Sehaltiel, Aphiel and Zarahiel, at the command of Orifiel, depart from us Moloch! We deny thee our children to devour.

The Circle is now closed with the banishing pentagrams of all four elements.

Consecrating Talismans

The following is an example of a simple ritual used in consecrating or charging talismans and is borrowed from my first teacher who, in turn, based them upon rituals found in The Arbatel. Where I've inserted (S) in the ritual it means that at this point you would trace the appropriate sign, seal or sigil in the air using the wand. (A good source for finding these is *The Golden Dawn*.) For other planets you'd need to change the invoking pentagram, depending on where the planet is at the time, change the names of the entities summoned, of course, and use the sigils and signs appropriate to those entities.

Conjuration of Mercury
Consecration of Mercury Talisman

1. Establish the circle as you usually would, beginning with the LBR. Invoke the element of the astrological sign Mercury is in at the time using the Invoking Pentagram in the proper quadrant (direction). If you need to, do a banishing for the element of any sign which is in an aspect to Mercury that might interfere or even work directly against you, using the Banishing Pentagram in its proper place.

Next, make the Invoking Hexagram of Mercury as shown in figure 2 on page 242.

2. Perform the proper Solar Adoration and/or the basic Preliminary Invocation of your own preference.

3. Mentally charge the circle with the appropriate element to be invoked and with the appropriate color.

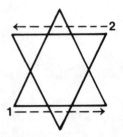

Figure 2. Invoking Hexagram of Mercury.

4. Next, proceed with the invocation itself, either borrowing one from a book or making up your own. (It doesn't need to be as elaborate as the one used for conjuring an elemental.) You can use any Mercurial intelligence, spirit, angel, etc. In this case we're using the Olympic Spirit Ophiel, and since Mercury was in an air sign at the time, the appropriate Hebrew and Enochian names are used for the kings.

I adjure thee, in the name of Shaddai El Chai, and in the name of Oro Ibam Aozpi, the divine names which rule the quarter of the heavens wherein thou reside at this time, and in the name of Raphael and further Bataivam the King of the Airey Domain;

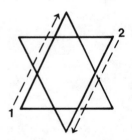

Figure 3. Banishing Hexagram of Mercury.

further Chassan, Ariel and Paralda, thy chiefs. I adjure thee that thou mayest send thine Intelligence Tiriel whose seal I draw (S) and Taphthartharath whose seal I draw (S) to hasten to come and consecrate these talismans into potent, living symbols of thy living force of Hod, thine essence. Bestow upon them life and thy power. May they vibrate to the innermost realms and shake loose the foundations of the obstacles to thy will. In the name of Shaddai El Chai arise! Move! and Appear! Be thou obedient unto me, for I am the master of the forces of matter, the servant of the same thy God is my name, true worshipper of the highest! (Knock or ring the bell eight times.)

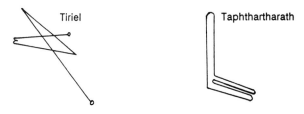

Tiriel

Taphthartharath

5. Mentally charge the circle with the Mercurial Sigil; that is, impress it upon the altar and the talismans. Once you're certain of a positive result, turn the talismans over on their faces or cover them with a cloth so that when you proceed to do the banishings you won't banish the energy in the talismans as well.

6. The License to Depart

Because thou camest in peace and quietness in answer to my command and did send thine Intelligences and Spirits as I required of thee, I give thee and thine license to depart. Go in peace and quit this circle. Return to thy domain in the silence, but only come again should I again require thee, and by thy name and seal to conjure thee. Go in peace.

7. Do the Banishing Hexagram of Mercury as shown in figure 3, and close the circle.

Suppliers

Following is a short list of some companies that sell books and supplies by mail. It's not complete, but it should provide a starting point.

Circle
P.O. Box 9013
Madison, WI 53715

Little Shop of Incense
6207 North Broadway
Chicago, IL 60660

Llwellyn Publishers
P.O. Box 64383
St. Paul, MN 55164-0383

Magickal Blend
P.O. Box 11303
San Francisco, CA 94101

Magickal Childe
35 W. 19th Street
New York, NY 10011

Mysteria Products Co.
Div. of Dorene Publishing Co., Inc.
P.O. Box 1466
Arlington, TX 76004

Occult Digest
International Imports
8050 Webb Ave.
North Hollywood, CA 91605

Rondo's Temple Sales
171 Mitchell St., S.W.
Atlanta, GA 30303

Tyrad Company
Box 17006
Minneapolis, MN 55417

Samuel Weiser, Inc.
132 E. 24th Street
New York, NY 10010

Worldwide Curio House
P.O. Box 17095
Minneapolis, MN 55417

Bibliography

The Arbatel

Adler, Margot. *Drawing Down the Moon*. Boston: Beacon Press, 1987.

Aldington, Richard and Delano Ames (Tr.). *New Larousse Encyclopedia of Mythology*. NYC: Prometheus Press, 1974.

Bardon, Franz. *Initiation Into Hermetics*.

Barrett, Francis. *The Magus*. Secaucus, NJ: The Citadel Press, 1967.

Buckland, Raymond. *Practical Candle-Burning Rituals*. St. Paul, MN: Llewellyn Publications, 1984.

———. *The Tree*. York Beach, ME: Samuel Weiser, Inc., 1974.

———. *Witchcraft From The Inside*. St. Paul, MN: Llewellyn Publications, 1971.

Budge, E.A. Wallis. *Egyptian Magic*. Secaucas, NJ: Citadel Press, 1978.

Castaneda, Carlos. *The Teachings of Don Juan, A Yaqui Way of Knowledge*. New York: Pocket Books, 1974.

———. *Tales of Power*. New York: Washington Square Press, 1974.

Crowley, Aleister. *Diary of a Drug Fiend*. York Beach, ME: Samuel Weiser, Inc., 1970.

———. *The Equinox*. York Beach, ME: Samuel Weiser, Inc., 1972.

————. *Magick in Theory and Practice*. New York: Dover Press, 1976.

Culpeper, Nicholas. *Complete Herbal*. Cedar Knolls, NJ: Wehman Bros., Inc., 1960.

Cunningham, Scott. *Cunningham's Encyclopedia of Magical Herbs*. St. Paul, MN: Llewellyn Publications, 1985.

————. *Earth Power: Techniques of Natural Magic*. St. Paul, MN: Llewellyn Publications, 1985.

————. *Magic of Incense, Oils and Brews*. St. Paul, MN: Llewellyn Publications, 1986.

————. *Magical Herbalism: The Secret Craft of the Wise*. St. Paul, MN: Llewellyn Publications, 1984.

Cunningham, Scott, and David Harrington. *Magical Household*. St. Paul, MN: Llewellyn Publications, 1987.

Davidson, Gustav. *Dictionary of Angels*. New York: Free Press, 1972.

de Laurence, Lauron W. *Lesser Key of Solomon (Goetia)*. Cedar Knolls, NJ: Wehman Bros., Inc.

Farrar, Stewart. *What Witches Do*. Custer, WA: Phoenix Publishing, Inc., 1983.

Fortune, Dion. *Moon Magick*. York Beach, ME: Samuel Weiser, Inc., 1979.

————. *Psychic Self-Defense*. York Beach, ME: Samuel Weiser, Inc., 1977.

————. *Sane Occultism*. York Beach, ME: Samuel Weiser, Inc., 1987.

————. *Sea Priestess*. York Beach, ME: Samuel Weiser, Inc., 1979.

————. *The Secrets of Dr. Taverner*. St. Paul, MN: Llewellyn Publications, 1979.

Frazer, James G. *The Golden Bough*. New York: Crown Publishers, Inc., 1981.

Gardner, Gerald. *High Magick's Aid*. York Beach, ME: Samuel Weiser, Inc., 1974.

————. *The Meaning of Witchcraft*. New York: Magickal Childe, 1982.

————. *Witchcraft Today*. Secaucas, NJ: Citadel Press, 1970.

Glass, Justine. *Witchcraft The Sixth Sense*. N. Hollywood, CA: Wilshire Book Co.

Graves, Sir Robert. *The White Goddess*. New York: Farrar, Straus & Giroux, Inc., 1966.

Hall, Manly P. *Blessed Angels*. Los Angeles: Philosophical Research Society.

Holzer, Hans. *New Pagans*. Garden City, NY: Doubleday & Co., 1972.

Huson, Paul. *Mastering Witchcraft*. New York: Putnam Publishing Group, 1980.

Johns, June. *King of the Witches*. New York: Coward-McCann, Inc., 1970.

Kloss, Jethro. *Back to Eden*. Loma Linda, CA: Back to Eden Books, 1985.

Leek, Sybil. *Diary of a Witch*. NY: New American Library, 1975. Book is out of print.

Leland, Charles. *Aradia: The Gospel of the Witches*. London: The C.W. Daniel Company, 1974.

Lethridge, Thomas C. *Witches*. Secaucus, NJ: Citadel Press, 1969.

Levi, Eliphas. *Transcendental Magic*. York Beach, ME: Samuel Weiser, Inc., 1970.

Mathers, S. Liddell MacGregor. *Key of Solomon the King*. York Beach, ME: Samuel Weiser, Inc., 1989.

Murray, Margaret Alice. *God of the Witches*. New York: Oxford University Press, Inc., 1974.

————. *Witch-cult in Western Europe*. Oxford, UK: Oxford University Press, 1971.

Pond, David, and Lucy Pond. *Metaphysical Handbook*. Port Ludlow, WA: Reflecting Pond Publications.

Regardie, Israel. *The Golden Dawn*. St. Paul, MN: Llewellyn Publications, 1971.

Roman, Sanaya, and Duane Packer. *Opening to Channel: How to Connect with your Guide*. Tiburon, CA: H.J. Kramer, Inc. 1987.

Ross, Anne. *Pagan Celtic Britain.*

Scott, Cyril. *The Initiate.* York Beach, ME: Samuel Weiser, Inc., 1977.

Spence, Lewis. *Encyclopedia of Occultism.* Secaucus, NJ: Citadel Press, 1984.

Starhawk. *Dreaming the Dark: Magic, Sex and Politics.* Boston: Beacon Press, 1989.

————. *Spiral Dance.* New York: Harper & Row, 1989.

Valiente, Doreen. *ABC of Witchcraft Past and Present.* Custer, WA: Phoenix Publishing, Inc., 1984.

————. *Witchcraft for Tomorrow.* Custer, WA: Phoenix Publishing, Inc., 1983.